Get Fit!

The Personal Trainer for Academic Teams

By Randy Thompson

Incentive Publications, Inc.
Nashville, Tennessee

For Debra

Acknowledgements

I would like to acknowledge all of the principals, schools, and school districts that I have had the opportunity to know and work with over the years. They have allowed me to see practical strategies at work and observe positive changes. These would be represented by, but are not limited to, the following schools: Boca Ciega High School, Maybele Vale Middle Magnet School, Rayville Middle School, Alexandria Middle School, Wrightstown Middle School; school districts: Rapides Parish Schools and Richland Parish Schools in Louisiana, Omaha Public Schools in Nebraska, Little Rock Public Schools in Arkansas; and, of course, many principals: Walt Grebing, Glenn Purpura, Ann Blaylock, Rich Schenkus, Paula Nelson, and Jim Greule.

Illustrated by Kathleen Bullock
Cover by Geoffrey Brittingham
Edited by Jill Norris
Copy edited by Cary Grayson

ISBN 978-0-86530-713-1

1 2 3 4 5 6 7 8 9 10 11 10 09 08

PRINTED IN THE UNITED STATES OF AMERICA
www.incentivepublications.com

Table of Contents

Taking the Teaming Assessment

Personal trainers work with people to help them self-assess their strengths and weaknesses in order to determine what areas they need and want to develop. After an initial assessment, the personal trainer puts together a customized fitness program specifically for each individual. The ultimate goal for anyone enlisting the assistance of a personal trainer is to get as fit as possible overall. The personal trainer provides a series of exercises and a schedule of how often each of the exercises should be done. Trainers teach the mechanics and proper form for each exercise to maximize the impact of every movement. Most people do not have unlimited time to work out, so the personal trainer creates an agenda to help them get the most out of every minute they can put into working out. Finally, the personal trainer is an expert in motivation and is able to help people with mental preparation as well as physical development.

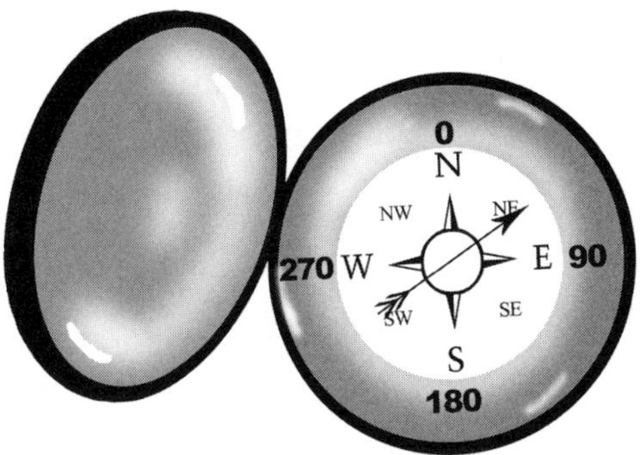

Academic teams who wish to get fit and be the best they can be must first determine where they are currently by taking the teaming assessment. Then, team members use the appropriate activities in the book to maximize their effectiveness in the areas where improvement is needed.

Using the Self Assessment

The "Teaming Assessment" (pages 10–17) is matched to the training manual *Get Fit!* Academic teams self-assess their strengths and weaknesses. *Get Fit!* provides instruction and practice for improving any weaknesses that are identified. The ultimate goal is for every team to be as fit as possible in all areas of the assessment.

The teaming assessment is a self-assessment. It can and should be used by both core and exploratory teams. With the help of the assessment, each team will decide where their strengths are and then determine the areas they want to improve. Each section of the assessment and the book will stand alone and is intended to help teams focus on the specific tasks for that area. In fact, each item within each area of the assessment can stand alone as well. Each of the individual items in the assessment is cross-referenced to the specific page numbers in the book that discuss that competency.

If your team does not score well on any individual item, and would like to improve, reference that part of the chapter indicated in the book to develop that specific skill. If a team doesn't score well overall for an entire section of the assessment, then the team might consider making the entire chapter a part of its professional development. So, your team can work on one item at a time within an assessment category, or look at the overall category and choose to work on all of the skills gradually, but simultaneously. The chapters in the book are organized around the assessment categories, and are intended to help teams improve their efforts in areas of their choosing.

This assessment is very comprehensive and may cover areas that are not available to some teams, or at all in some schools. For example, not all teams or schools will have a flexible block schedule, so such a team would not be able to do any of the examples listed in that part of the assessment. That is another reason why each part of the assessment is meant to stand alone. Teams should only work on the parts of the assessment that pertain to their circumstances. However, schools might review sections that currently do not apply to their situation. *(They may not know what they are missing!)*

Do not read this book from front to back! You and your team will want to focus on the categories that you are most interested in developing. It is very much OK for you and your team to skip around in the book, reviewing skills as needed. If your school is just moving into teaming, your teams will not be doing all of the things listed in this assessment from the beginning. Enjoy the possibilities as your team uses the personal trainer to get better and better.

If you have been in teams for a while, and your team does not score well in some of the areas, do not despair. Remember, the goal is continual improvement. As you will see throughout this book, I stress that teams must become professional learning communities—every team must engage in professional development during team meetings. This personal trainer's manual will facilitate the discussions that lead to developing and sharing even more effective strategies to maximize every team's efforts.

Practical Teaming Strategies

You will also see that the assessment and the book focus only on the practical aspects of teams. Each area of the assessment and the corresponding area of the book pinpoint practical tasks teams can do to enhance teaching and learning. Everything in the book is research-based, but this book centers on the tasks that teams do to put the research into practice. All the examples of activities shared in this book are currently being practiced in schools around the country.

Use the assessment on pages 10–17 as a diagnostic tool to identify skills in need of improvement. Then use the rest of the book as the prescriptive component to develop those areas. The "TAG, You're It!" section at the end of each chapter provides practical exercises to put the chapter's pedagogy into practice.

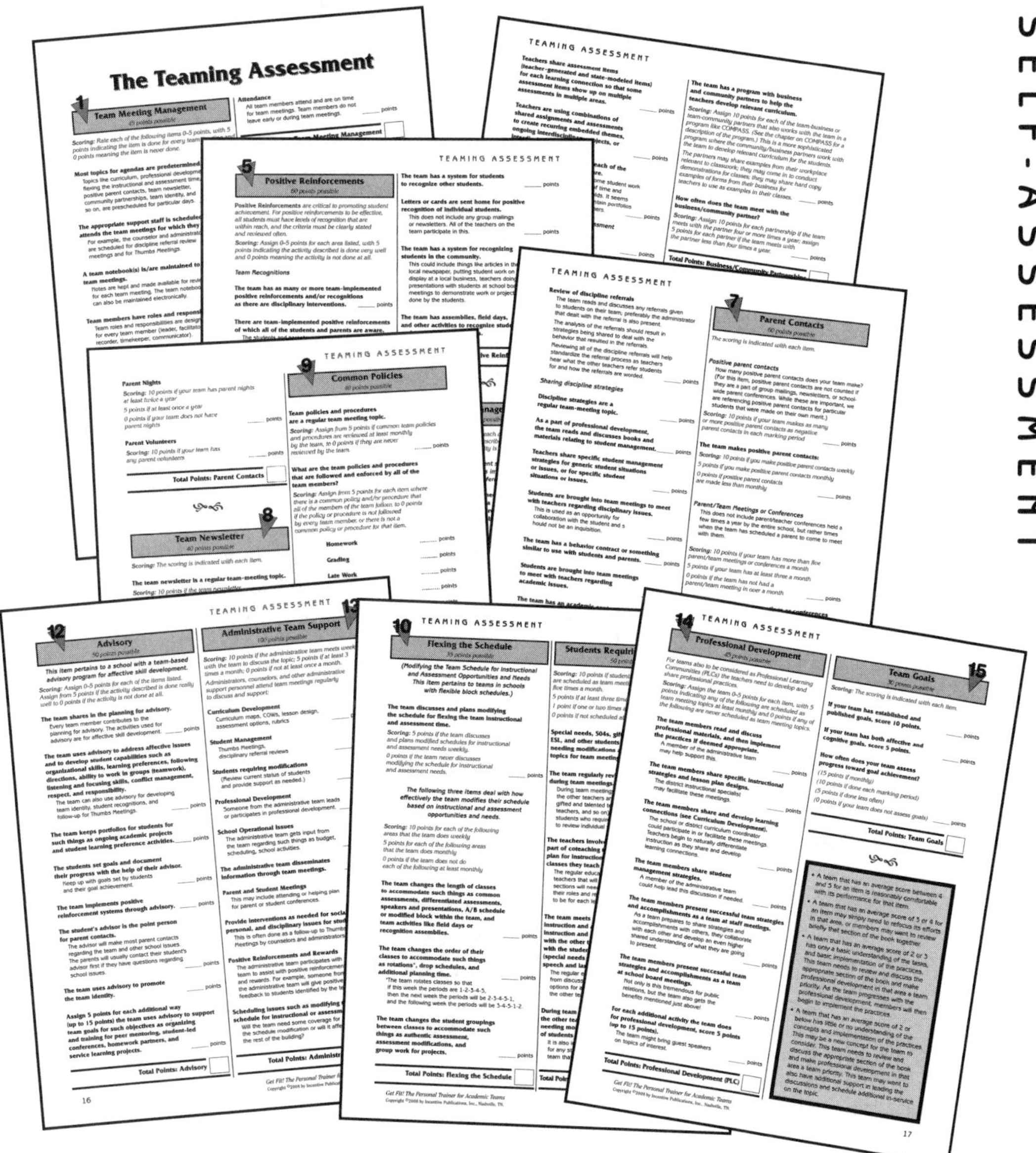

The Teaming Assessment

Team Meeting Management

45 points possible

Scoring: Rate each of the following items 0–5 points, with 5 points indicating the item is done for every team meeting and 0 points meaning the item is never done.

Most topics for agendas are predetermined.
Topics like curriculum, professional development, flexing the instructional and assessment time, positive parent contacts, team newsletter, community partnerships, team identity, and so on, are prescheduled for particular days. ______ points

The appropriate support staff is scheduled for and attends the team meetings for which they are needed.
For example, the counselor and administrator are scheduled for discipline referral review meetings and for *Thumbs Meetings*. ______ points

A team notebook(s) is/are maintained to document team meetings.
Notes are kept and made available for review for each team meeting. The team notebook can also be maintained electronically. ______ points

Team members have roles and responsibilities.
Team roles and responsibilities are designated for every team member (leader, facilitator, recorder, timekeeper, communicator). ______ points

Personal Responsibilities (PRs) are assigned as needed and then summarized after each team meeting.
Responsibilities for team tasks are distributed evenly between all team members. ______ points

Time Management—Staying on Task
The team stays on task and does not stray off topic. Time limits are assigned and adhered to for team meeting topics. ______ points

A team calling/contact log is maintained.
Teams need to document calls and other interactions (positive or negative), even in those instances where a message was left or no one answered the phone. ______ points

Meeting Place
Everyone knows where team meetings are going to be held, and the meeting place is appropriate for a team meeting. (Needed materials such as curriculum maps are provided; teachers have working room such as table space, etc.) ______ points

Attendance
All team members attend and are on time for team meetings. Team members do not leave early or during team meetings. ______ points

Total Points: Team Meeting Management ☐

Curriculum Development

55 points possible

Scoring: For each area below assign 0–5 points, with 5 points indicating the activity described is done every week and 0 points meaning the activity described is not done at all.

All team members participate in finding and developing interdisciplinary learning connections as follows:

Teachers reference specific skills in one class to demonstrate to students how they are used in another class.
When students ask "When are we ever going to use this?" the teacher can answer the question with regard to when and how the skill has been or will be used in other classes. ______ points

Teachers share overheads, computer slideshow files, worksheets, and activities so that they are used in context in multiple classes. ______ points

Teachers assign guided choice assignments based on work done in other classes.
For example: The language arts teacher assigns a descriptive writing exercise and chooses things for students to describe from topics covered in the other core and exploratory classes. ______ points

Teachers give students extra credit for work done in classes other than their own for skills that relate to both classes.
From the example just above: If the student chose to describe something from the math class, the math teacher would give the student extra credit, as would the science teacher or the art teacher and so on had the student chosen to write about their class. ______ points

Teachers share assessment items (teacher-generated and state-modeled items) for each learning connection so that some assessment items show up on multiple assessments in multiple areas. ______ points

Teachers are using combinations of shared assignments and assessments to create recurring embedded themes, ongoing interdisciplinary projects, or interdisciplinary units. ______ points

Portfolios are maintained for each of the students that the teachers share.

Ongoing projects require that some student work will be kept over a long period of time and accumulated as the project unfolds. It seems to work best if the students maintain portfolios with the assistance of their teachers. ______ points

Coordinate Homework and Assessment

Teachers know each other's homework assignments. ______ points

Teachers coordinate with each other to make sure cumulative homework amounts are appropriate. ______ points

Teachers post homework in other classes and/or remind students of homework for other classes daily. ______ points

Teachers coordinate their assessments. ______ points

Total Points: Curriculum Development [ ]

Business/Community Partnerships

30 points possible

Scoring: *There will be a separate total for each business/community partnership a team has.*

The team has one or more traditional team-business or team-community partnerships.

Scoring: *Assign 10 points for each traditional team-business or team-community partnership the team has developed. The traditional partnership usually involves the donation of time and/or money to the team from a business or community organization.* ______ points

The team has a program with business and community partners to help the teachers develop relevant curriculum.

Scoring: *Assign 10 points for each of the team-business or team-community partners that also works with the team in a program like COMPASS. (See the chapter on COMPASS for a description of the program.) This is a more sophisticated program where the community/business partners work with the team to develop relevant curriculum for the students.*

The partners may share examples from their workplace relevant to classwork; they may come in to conduct demonstrations for classes; they may share hard copy examples of forms from their business for teachers to use as examples in their classes. ______ points

How often does the team meet with the business/community partner?

Scoring: *Assign 10 points for each partnership if the team meets with the partner four or more times a year; assign 5 points for each partner if the team meets with the partner less than four times a year.* ______ points

Total Points: Business/Community Partnerships [ ]

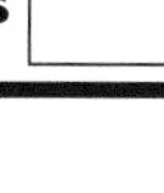

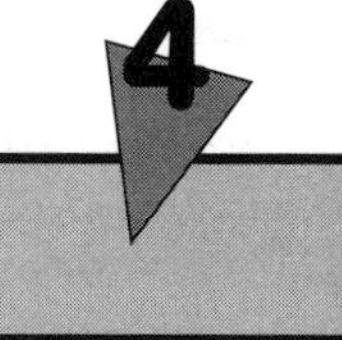

Team Identity

35 points possible

Scoring: *The scoring is indicated in each item.*

The team has a team name that every student and parent knows.

Scoring: *Assign 0–5 points. Assign from 0 points, indicating your team does not have a team name, up to 5 points, depending on how much time and effort the team puts into developing its team identity.* ______ points

Give the team 5 points for each thing the team does to prominently reinforce the team identity up to 30 points total. This would include such things as team logo, team banners, team displays in the cafeteria, team T-shirts, team newsletter, team name on assignments and projects, team assemblies, team recognitions. (One team told me they had a team banner but did not know where it was. This certainly would not count!) ______ points

Total Points: Team Identity [ ]

Positive Reinforcements

60 points possible

Positive Reinforcements *are critical to promoting student achievement. For positive reinforcements to be effective, all students must have levels of recognition that are within reach, and the criteria must be clearly stated and reviewed often.*

Scoring: *Assign 0–5 points for each area listed, with 5 points indicating the activity described is done very well and 0 points meaning the activity is not done at all.*

Team Recognitions

The team has as many or more team-implemented positive reinforcements and/or recognitions as there are disciplinary interventions. ______ points

There are team-implemented positive reinforcements of which all of the students and parents are aware.
The students and parents are aware of the reward and recognition systems and the criteria involved. ______ points

The positive reinforcements are designed to impact all students.
Positive reinforcements and rewards do not impact students that cannot achieve them; therefore, the team has tiered positive reinforcements and rewards. For instance, students may contribute to the team's increased GPA. This way the student that improves his or her grades in any increment in any class has contributed to increasing the team GPA. ______ points

The team displays examples of student work. ______ points

The team informs administrators of student accomplishments for recognition from the administrators. ______ points

The team recognizes affective achievements as well as cognitive achievements.
This could include recognition for students who might: work as a peer mentor, help other students with homework, help with hallway decorations or clean-up, and so on. ______ points

The team has a system for sharing student accomplishments from any one class to be used as a positive reinforcement in all the classes.
For example: a student does a good job on a math assignment, and the next day every teacher on the team is congratulating the student for the work he or she did in math class. ______ points

Students are brought into team meetings to receive praise for accomplishments. ______ points

The team has a system for students to recognize other students. ______ points

Letters or cards are sent home for positive recognition of individual students.
This does not include any group mailings or newsletters. All of the teachers on the team participate in this. ______ points

The team has a system for recognizing students in the community.
This could include things like articles in the local newspaper, putting student work on display at a local business, teachers doing presentations with students at school board meetings to demonstrate work or projects done by the students. ______ points

The team has assemblies, field days, and other activities to recognize student and team accomplishments. ______ points

Total Points: Positive Reinforcement ☐

Student Management

60 points possible

Scoring: *Assign 0–5 points for each area below, with 5 points indicating the activity described is done very well and 0 points meaning the activity is not done at all.*

Proactive student management strategies are used. These are interventions implemented prior to students receiving referrals. For example:

Thumbs Meetings or similar meetings are conducted at least two times a month to identify students needing interventions and/or additional support for behavior or academic concerns. ______ points

Administrators and counselors meet with teams weekly to get information so they can be involved with students as issues are developing and prior to students receiving referrals. ______ points

Parent contacts are made early in the student intervention process as issues are developing and are still in the prereferral stage. ______ points

Review of discipline referrals

The team reads and discusses any referrals given to students on their team; preferably the administrator that dealt with the referral is also present.

The analysis of the referrals should result in strategies being shared to deal with the behavior that resulted in the referrals.

Reviewing all of the discipline referrals will help standardize the referral process as teachers hear what the other teachers refer students for and how the referrals are worded. ______ points

Sharing discipline strategies

Discipline strategies are a regular team-meeting topic. ______ points

As a part of professional development, the team reads and discusses books and materials relating to student management. ______ points

Teachers share specific student management strategies for generic student situations or issues, or for specific student situations or issues. ______ points

Students are brought into team meetings to meet with teachers regarding disciplinary issues.

This is used as an opportunity for collaboration with the student and s hould not be an inquisition. ______ points

The team has a behavior contract or something similar to use with students and parents. ______ points

Students are brought into team meetings to meet with teachers regarding academic issues. ______ points

The team has an academic contract or something similar to use with students and parents. ______ points

The team shares and discusses specific classroom instructional strategies that address classroom management issues at least monthly.

The team discusses how different students respond to different classroom situations and how to design instruction to avoid student management issues with certain students. ______ points

Total Points: Student Management [ ]

Parent Contacts

60 points possible

The scoring is indicated with each item.

Positive parent contacts

How many positive parent contacts does your team make? (For this item, positive parent contacts are not counted if they are a part of group mailings, newsletters, or school-wide parent conferences. While these are important, we are referencing positive parent contacts for particular students that were made on their own merit.)

Scoring: *10 points if your team makes as many or more positive parent contacts as negative parent contacts in each marking period* ______ points

The team makes positive parent contacts:

Scoring: *10 points if you make positive parent contacts weekly*

5 points if you make positive parent contacts monthly

0 points if positive parent contacts are made less than monthly ______ points

Parent/Team Meetings or Conferences

This does not include parent/teacher conferences held a few times a year by the entire school, but rather times when the team has scheduled a parent to come to meet with them.

Scoring: *10 points if your team has more than five parent/team meetings or conferences a month*

5 points if your team has at least three a month

0 points if the team has not had a parent/team meeting in over a month ______ points

Planning for parent/team meetings or conferences

Scoring: *ranging from 5 points (if your team preplans for parent meetings) to 0 points (if the team does not plan for parent meetings)*

Planning means more than just setting the date and time. Planning means that the team has a game plan going into the parent meeting and has discussed things like who is going to facilitate, identifying the issues, the focus issue, possible solutions, who is going to follow up with the parent after the meeting, and so on. ______ points

Follow-up for Parent/Team Meetings or Conferences

Scoring: *ranging from 5 points (if the team does a follow-up contact for all parent meetings) to 0 points (if the team does not contact parents after all parent conferences)*

Someone from the team calls some time after the parent/team meeting to let the parents know how their child is doing as a result of the discussion and decisions made at the meeting. ______ points

Parent Nights

Scoring: *10 points if your team has parent nights at least twice a year*

5 points if at least once a year

0 points if your team does not have parent nights ______ points

Parent Volunteers

Scoring: *10 points if your team has any parent volunteers* ______ points

Total Points: Parent Contacts [ ]

8 Team Newsletter

40 points possible

Scoring: *The scoring is indicated with each item.*

The team newsletter is a regular team-meeting topic.

Scoring: *10 points if the team newsletter is a weekly team-meeting topic.*

5 points if the team newsletter is at least a monthly team-meeting topic.

0 points if the team newsletter is not ever a scheduled team meeting topic. ______ points

How many times each year is a team newsletter produced and distributed?

Scoring: *15 points if newsletter is distributed monthly or more*

10 points if every marking period

5 points if once a semester

0 points if there is no team newsletter ______ points

How many times each year does your team put something in the local newspaper?

Scoring: *15 points if monthly or more*

10 points if every marking period

5 points if once a semester

0 points if the team does not put anything in the local newspaper ______ points

Total Points: Newsletter/Newspaper [ ]

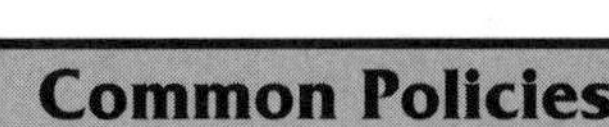

9 Common Policies

40 points possible

Team policies and procedures are a regular team meeting topic.

Scoring: *Assign from 5 points if common team policies and procedures are reviewed at least monthly by the team, to 0 points if they are never reviewed by the team.* ______ points

What are the team policies and procedures that are followed and enforced by all of the team members?

Scoring: *Assign from 5 points for each item where there is a common policy and/or procedure that all of the members of the team follow, to 0 points if the policy or procedure is not followed by every team member, or there is not a common policy or procedure for that item.*

Homework ______ points

Grading ______ points

Late Work ______ points

Tardy ______ points

Paper Headings ______ points

For additional common team policies and procedures addressing such things as bathroom passes, gum chewing, food and drink in the classes, and dress code, add up to 10 points. ______ points

Total Points: Common Policies [ ]

"Failure to prepare is preparing to fail."
Coach John Wooden

Flexing the Schedule

35 points possible

(Modifying the Team Schedule for Instructional and Assessment Opportunities and Needs This item pertains to teams in schools with flexible block schedules.)

The team discusses and plans modifying the schedule for flexing the team instructional and assessment time.

Scoring: 5 points if the team discusses and plans modified schedules for instructional and assessment needs weekly.

0 points if the team never discusses modifying the schedule for instructional and assessment needs. ______ points

The following three items deal with how effectively the team modifies their schedule based on instructional and assessment opportunities and needs.

Scoring: 10 points for each of the following areas that the team does weekly

5 points for each of the following areas that the team does monthly

0 points if the team does not do each of the following at least monthly

The team changes the length of classes to accommodate such things as common assessments, differentiated assessments, speakers and presentations, A/B schedule or modified block within the team, and team activities like field days or recognition assemblies. ______ points

The team changes the order of their classes to accommodate such things as rotations*, drop schedules, and additional planning time. ______ points

*The team rotates classes so that if this week the periods are 1-2-3-4-5, then the next week the periods will be 2-3-4-5-1, and the following week the periods will be 3-4-5-1-2.

The team changes the student groupings between classes to accommodate such things as authentic assessment, assessment modifications, and group work for projects. ______ points

Total Points: Flexing the Schedule ☐

Students Requiring Modifications

50 points possible

Scoring: 10 points if students needing modifications are scheduled as team meeting topics more than five times a month.

5 points if at least three times a month.

1 point if one or two times a month.

0 points if not scheduled at least once a month.

Special needs, 504s, gifted and talented, ESL, and other students identified as needing modifications are prescheduled topics for team meetings. ______ points

The team regularly reviews IEPs, pre-IEPs, and 504s during team meetings.

During team meetings, the team regularly confers with the other teachers and staff (special needs teachers, gifted and talented teachers, speech and language teachers, and so on) assigned to work with the students who require modifications to review individual student progress. ______ points

The teachers involved with inclusion that are part of coteaching teams meet regularly to plan for instruction and assessment for the classes they teach together.

The regular education and the special needs teachers that will be coteaching inclusion sections will need to plan together for what their roles and responsibilities are going to be for each lesson. ______ points

The team meets regularly to work on general instruction and assessment options (differentiated instruction and authentic assessment for all classes) with the other teachers and staff assigned to work with the students with required modifications (special needs teachers, gifted and talented teachers, speech and language teachers).

The regular education teachers will benefit from discussing instruction and assessment options for all classes while working with the other teachers listed above. ______ points

During team meetings, the team regularly meets with the other teachers and staff working with the students needing modifications to review individual progress of students that do not have IEPs.

It is also important to identify, discuss, and plan for any students that do not have IEPs on the team that would benefit from modifications. ______ points

Total Points: Students Requiring Modifications ☐

Advisory

50 points possible

This item pertains to a school with a team-based advisory program for affective skill development.

Scoring: *Assign 0–5 points for each of the items listed. Assign from 5 points if the activity described is done really well to 0 points if the activity is not done at all.*

The team shares in the planning for advisory.
Every team member contributes to the planning for advisory. The activities used for advisory are for affective skill development. ______ points

The team uses advisory to address affective issues and to develop student capabilities such as organizational skills, learning preferences, following directions, ability to work in groups (teamwork), listening and focusing skills, conflict management, respect, and responsibility.
The team can also use advisory for developing team identity, student recognitions, and follow-up for Thumbs Meetings. ______ points

The team keeps portfolios for students for such things as ongoing academic projects and student learning preference activities. ______ points

The students set goals and document their progress with the help of their advisor.
Keep up with goals set by students and their goal achievement. ______ points

The team implements positive reinforcement systems through advisory. ______ points

The student's advisor is the point person for parent contacts.
The advisor will make most parent contacts regarding the team and other school issues. The parents will usually contact their student's advisor first if they have questions regarding school issues. ______ points

The team uses advisory to promote the team identity. ______ points

Assign 5 points for each additional way (up to 15 points) the team uses advisory to support team goals for such objectives as organizing and training for peer mentoring, student-led conferences, homework partners, and service learning projects. ______ points

Total Points: Advisory ☐

13 Administrative Team Support

100 points possible

Scoring: *10 points if the administrative team meets weekly with the team to discuss the topic; 5 points if at least 3 times a month; 0 points if not at least once a month.*

Administrators, counselors, and other administrative support personnel attend team meetings regularly to discuss and support:

Curriculum Development
Curriculum maps, COWs, lesson design, assessment options, rubrics ______ points

Student Management
Thumbs Meetings, disciplinary referral reviews ______ points

Students requiring modifications
(Review current status of students and provide support as needed.) ______ points

Professional Development
Someone from the administrative team leads or participates in professional development. ______ points

School Operational Issues
The administrative team gets input from the team regarding such things as budget, scheduling, school activities. ______ points

The administrative team disseminates information through team meetings. ______ points

Parent and Student Meetings
This may include attending or helping plan for parent or student conferences. ______ points

Provide interventions as needed for social, emotional, personal, and disciplinary issues for students.
This is often done as a follow-up to Thumbs Meetings by counselors and administrators. ______ points

Positive Reinforcements and Rewards
The administrative team participates with the team to assist with positive reinforcements and rewards. For example, someone from the administrative team will give positive feedback to students identified by the team. ______ points

Scheduling issues such as modifying the team schedule for instructional or assessment needs.
Will the team need some coverage for the schedule modification or will it affect the rest of the building? ______ points

Total Points: Administrative Team ☐

Professional Development

45 points possible

For teams also to be considered as Professional Learning Communities (PLCs) the teachers need to develop and share professional practices.

***Scoring:** Assign the team 0–5 points for each item, with 5 points indicating any of the following are scheduled as team meeting topics at least monthly and 0 points if any of the following are never scheduled as team meeting topics.*

The team members read and discuss professional materials, and then implement the practices if deemed appropriate.
A member of the administrative team may help support this. ______ points

The team members share specific instructional strategies and lesson plan designs.
The district instructional specialist may facilitate these meetings. ______ points

The team members share and develop learning connections (see Curriculum Development).
The school or district curriculum coordinator could participate in or facilitate these meetings. Teachers begin to naturally differentiate instruction as they share and develop learning connections. ______ points

The team members share student management strategies.
A member of the administrative team could help lead this discussion if needed. ______ points

The team members present successful team strategies and accomplishments as a team at staff meetings.
As a team prepares to share strategies and accomplishments with others, they collaborate with each other and develop an even higher shared understanding of what they are going to present. ______ points

The team members present successful team strategies and accomplishments as a team at school board meetings.
Not only is this tremendous for public relations, but the team also gets the benefits mentioned just above! ______ points

For each additional activity the team does for professional development, score 5 points (up to 15 points).
The team might bring guest speakers on topics of interest. ______ points

Total Points: Professional Development (PLC) ☐

15

Team Goals

30 points possible

***Scoring:** The scoring is indicated with each item.*

If your team has established and published goals, score 10 points. ______ points

If your team has both affective and cognitive goals, score 5 points. ______ points

How often does your team assess progress toward goal achievement?
(15 points if monthly)
(10 points if done each marking period)
(5 points if done less often)
(0 points if your team does not assess goals) ______ points

Total Points: Team Goals ☐

- A team that has an average score between 4 and 5 for an item is reasonably comfortable with its performance for that item.
- A team that has an average score of 3 or 4 for an item may simply need to refocus its efforts in that area, or members may want to review briefly that section of the book together.
- A team that has an average score of 2 or 3 has only a basic understanding of the tasks, and basic implementation of the practices. This team needs to review and discuss the appropriate section of the book and make professional development in that area a team priority. As the team progresses with the professional development, members will then begin to implement the practices.
- A team that has an average score of 2 or below has little or no understanding of the concepts and implementation of the practices. This may be a new concept for the team to consider. This team needs to review and discuss the appropriate section of the book and make professional development in that area a team priority. This team may want to also have additional support in leading the discussions and schedule additional in-service on the topic.

Scoring the Assessment

- A team that has an average score between 4 and 5 for an item is reasonably comfortable with its performance for that item.
- A team that has an average score of 3 or 4 for an item may simply need to refocus its efforts in that area, or members may want to review briefly that section of the book together.
- A team that has an average score of 2 or 3 has only a basic understanding of the tasks, and basic implementation of the practices. This team needs to review and discuss the appropriate section of the book and make professional development in that area a team priority. As the team progresses with the professional development, members will then begin to implement the practices.
- A team that has an average score of 2 or below has little or no understanding of the concepts and implementation of the practices. This may be a new concept for the team to consider. This team needs to review and discuss the appropriate section of the book and make professional development in that area a team priority. This team may want to also have additional support in leading the discussions and schedule additional in-service on the topic.

You Have a Team Score, Now What?

Once your team has completed and scored the teaming assessment, discuss your cumulative results. Think about the results.

- Were they what you expected?
- Were there any surprises?
- How would you summarize your overall results?

Just as you use formative assessment to determine what you need to teach your students, your team will now use the results of the teaming assessment to formulate a plan for improvement. *Get Fit!* will act as your personal trainer. Just follow these steps:

1) Select an area your team wants to address. Focus on one area and set a goal.
2) Consult the table of contents to find the chapter that matches the area you have chosen.
3) As a team, read and discuss the chapter.
4) Complete the "*TAG . . . You're It!*" exercises for the chapter you have read.
5) Put the skills and techniques into practice.

You may want to use an organizer such as the target on page 19 to help your team visualize the necessary steps, the timelines, and the personal responsibilities of team members. As you move toward your goal, you will become a professional learning community. You will develop and share best practice strategies to maximize your team's effectiveness.

Target Improvement

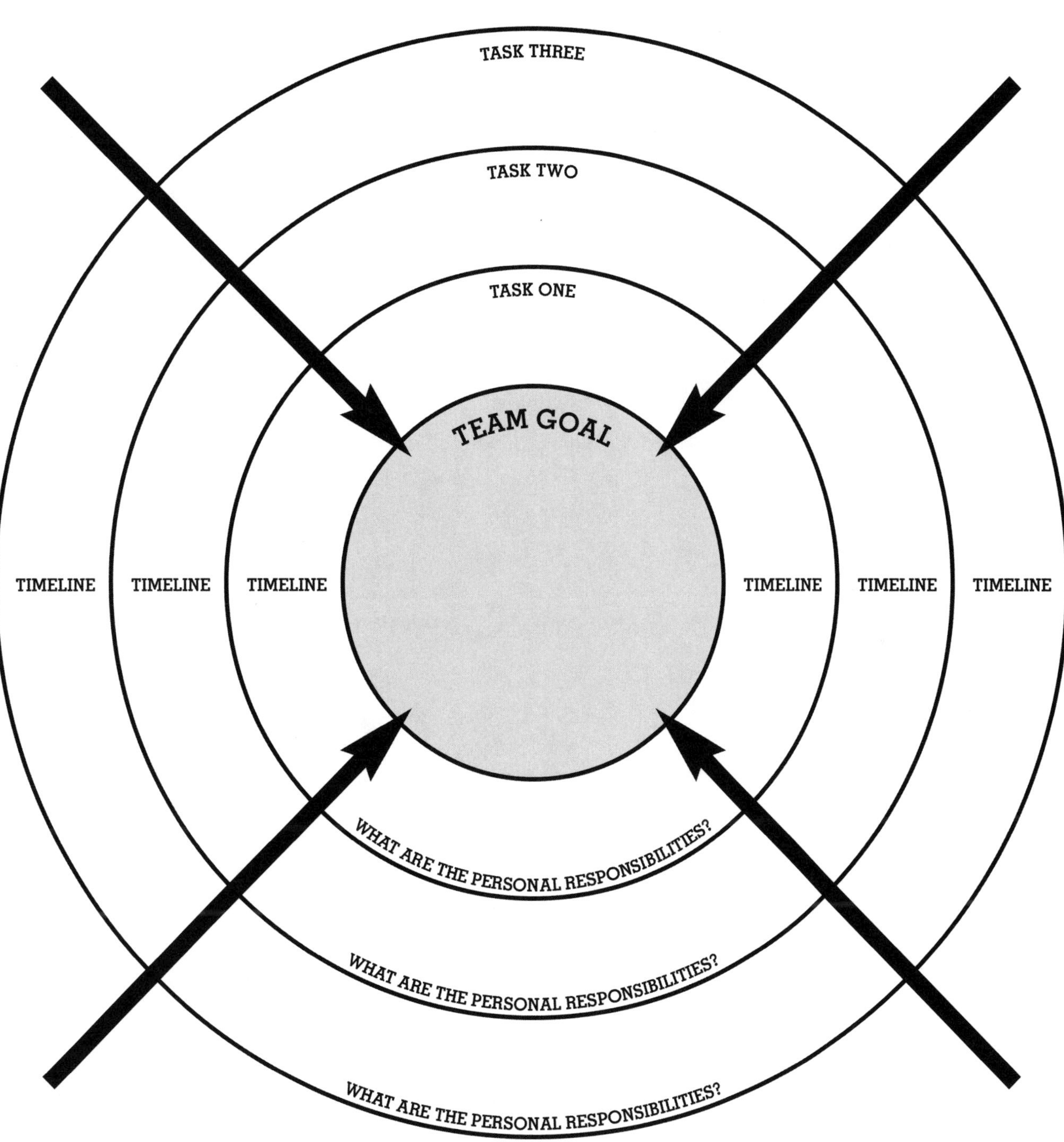

Interdisciplinary Team Management

Productive Team Meetings—Get Lean and Mean

People do not like to attend meetings where there is little direction and not much is accomplished. Productive team meetings are like circuit training in the gym. You want to move quickly between workout stations and you want to work hard at each station for a limited amount of time.

The purpose of this chapter is to help your team become more efficient and more effective. You will become the fly on the wall and look in at what happens during great team meetings. Regardless of the amount of time your team has to meet each week, this chapter will demonstrate how to get the most of every minute of team meetings.

Hopefully your team has a period every day to meet together, because, as you will see, teams need every minute they can get.

Focus on the practical things that teachers discuss and plan for during a team meeting. Each topic for a team meeting should have a direct impact on teaching and learning. All of the topics shared here should be regularly scheduled team meeting topics. Some should be discussed every week by the team, while others may be discussed several times a month.

My dad brought me up on "gottas" and "wannas." I would tell my dad that I had to do something, and he would often respond that I had my gottas and wannas mixed up. He would say, "You just wanna do that; you gotta mow the yard."

In this chapter, I am going to share how teams can deal with their "gottas" more effectively and efficiently, so that they can also get to their "wannas."

First, we will review what teams should be discussing during team time. The list that follows is fairly comprehensive, but it is a partial one at best. As you know, there is always more to discuss than there is time to meet. That is why teams often talk about feeling as if they are running on a treadmill. This chapter presents strategies that will help teams get to it all. Teachers work very hard all of the time, and sometimes they feel they do not move forward.

The following is a list of topics that teams should be addressing during team meetings.

THE "GOTTAS"

TEAM CALENDAR

- Coordinate tests, homework, etc.
- Plan for upcoming events

INDIVIDUAL STUDENT PROGRESS

- Academic issues
- Student management issues
- Proactive interventions for students
  - Thumbs Meetings to set up interventions for academic support, behavior issues, social, emotional, and personal issues.
- Share student learning styles information

PARENT CONTACTS

- Positive parent contacts
- Parents to be contacted for intervention purposes
- Information to be disseminated
  - Student information
  - Field trips, etc.
- Parent nights
- Volunteers

RECOGNITION PROGRAMS

- What are we doing as a team to systematically recognize student accomplishments?

ADVISORY

- Plan activities
- Manage student portfolios
  - Academic, goal setting. and achievement

FLEXING THE SCHEDULE

- Change the length of classes
  - Common tests, etc.
- Change the order of the classes
  - Run rotations
- Change the student groupings for classes
  - Project-driven schedule for a few days

FIELD TRIPS

- Buses, chaperones, permission slips, money

! STUDENTS REQUIRING MODIFICATIONS
- Discuss students with IEPs, 504s, ESL students, and so on
- Meet with the support personnel for these students
- Have Pre-IEPs

! CURRICULUM
- Curriculum mapping
  - Interdisciplinary learning connections discussion and development
  - Student projects
- Shared instructional strategies

! COMMUNITY AND BUSINESS PARTNERSHIPS
- Curriculum development with community and/or business partners

! NEWSLETTER
- Updates of classroom activities and team activities
- Monthly or at least each marking period

! TEAM IDENTITY
- Develop team name, assignments and projects, logo, T -shirts, banners, team building activities

! PROFESSIONAL DEVELOPMENT
- Shared readings
- Work with specialists in curriculum and instruction
- Shared strategies for classroom management and so on.

! COMMON POLICIES
- Decide on common policies for things like: paper headings, homework, grading, late work, and so on.

! REVIEW TEAM GOALS
- Set team goals
  - Both affective and cognitive
- Assess achievement of team goals

! SCHOOL BUSINESS
- Administrivia (There is always plenty of this to keep a team busy!)
  - Grades
  - All school assemblies or activities
  - School improvement forms and so on.

Getting to It All

That is quite a list of topics! With that much to do, and limited time to do it, just how in the world do teams get to it all? Great teams are the ones that know how to accomplish the most with the limited amount of time that they have. Team meetings that work share the following attributes:

- Meetings are scheduled.
- Members are on time.
- Everyone comes prepared.
- Meetings are comfortable and informal.
- Members agree to discuss issues, not people.
- Members work toward consensus.
- Agendas are accessible.
- Members stay on task.
- Most topics are prescheduled.
- Time limits are assigned and adhered to for each topic.
- A portion of the agenda is kept open.
- Members respect each other's differences.
- Roles and responsibilities are shared by all team members.
- Personal responsibilities (PRs) are assigned for tasks during each meeting and the PRs are summarized at the conclusion of each meeting.

Scheduling

Team meetings should be scheduled. Everyone should know in advance the time and the location of the meeting. Some teams have a specified team meeting room, but many teams meet in each other's classrooms. In that case, everyone needs to know which classroom they are meeting in each time. The team should also make sure that any support staff, such as administrators or counselors, who meet with the team know the meeting place and time.

It is important that everyone get to the team meeting on time. The two tricks to making sure that everyone shows up on time are to start on time, and to make sure that meetings are productive. If a team member knows that there is usually small talk for several minutes before the real team meeting starts, he or she will not be motivated to get to the meeting on time. Also, if team members view team time as wasted time where nothing gets done, then they are less likely to show up on time. Do not wait for someone who is late to start the team meeting; always start the team meeting on time. If you start on time every time, regardless of whether everyone is there or not, people will show up on time.

Agendas

The agenda is where it all starts. I like to have teams use a simple agenda form like the one on page 27. The framework includes space for personal responsibilities (PRs) and timelines, which enhance team productivity.

Use the agenda not only to plan for the meeting, but also to record what happened. At the top of the agenda, the recorder for the team lists members present. The "item" is the topic to be discussed. The word "period" stands for the amount of time that is going to be designated for each topic. My experience has been that five minutes seems to work well for each period. So if a topic is given three periods, that means the team is going to take fifteen minutes to discuss that topic. The recorder notes what action was taken for the topic under "discussion."

The team will divide whatever team meeting time they have to work with by five to get the number of periods available. A fifty-minute team meeting time will have ten periods. *Please note that I suggest teams always attempt to keep the last period open. That will give the team a five-minute cushion as teachers will need time to use the restroom, get back to class, and get ready for the next group of students.*

I suggest that teams use something such as a wind-up egg timer to time each topic. If a topic gets two periods, the timekeeper will set the timer to ten minutes and start the topic. The key to success is keeping on track—when the timer goes off, the team must move on to the next topic.

Personal Responsibilities and Time Management

Finally, the team determines who is going to be personally responsible for each task, and it records this personal responsibility (PR) on the agenda. When teams list and then summarize the personal responsibilities for each meeting, the team can see if the work is being distributed evenly. Sometimes in teams, one or two of the team members will end up with the bulk of the tasks. Having teams summarize the PRs at the end of each team meeting seems to help address this issue.

It is important to designate a timeline for each task along with the PR. That way, it is clear what is to be done, who is to do it, and when it is to be done. Without a clearly stated timeline for each task, tasks are put off (*Not that I would ever do something like that!*) or not done at all when someone forgets. If the team decides the timeline for the task is one week, they should go ahead and put the task on the following week's agenda to check on the progress. That is a sure way to assure the task gets done and the responsible team member will be ready to share what was done at the appropriate upcoming team meeting.

Sample Agendas

Note that the three sample agendas have their own style, but they all have the elements of effective agendas. Agendas help teams stay on task, and everyone feels productive. Try the basic agenda on page 27 and adapt it to your specific needs.

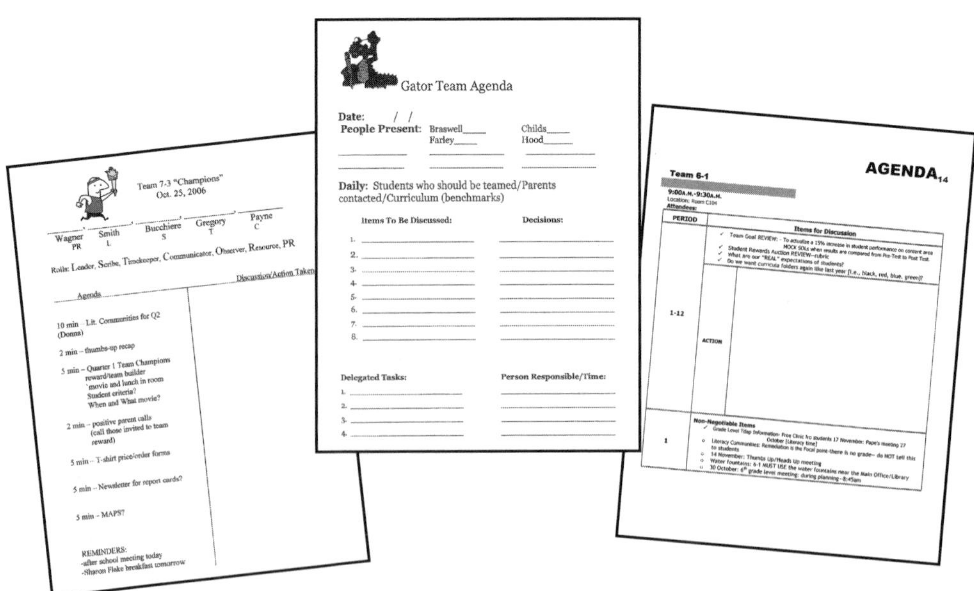

Team 7-3 "Champions"
Oct. 25, 2006

Wagner PR, Smith L, Bucchiere S, Gregory T, Payne C

Roles: Leader, Scribe, Timekeeper, Communicator, Observer, Resource, PR

Agenda — Discussion/Action Taken

10 min Lit. Communities for Q2 (Donna)
2 min – thumbs-up recap
5 min – Quarter 1 Team Champions reward/team builder 'movie and lunch in room Student criteria? When and What movie?
2 min – positive parent calls (call those invited to team reward)
5 min – T-shirt price/order forms
5 min – Newsletter for report cards?
5 min – MAPS?

REMINDERS:
-after school meeting today
-Sharon Flake breakfast tomorrow

Gator Team Agenda

Date: / /
People Present: Braswell___ Childs___ Farley___ Hood___

Daily: Students who should be teamed/Parents contacted/Curriculum (benchmarks)

Items To Be Discussed: 1.–8.
Decisions:

Delegated Tasks: 1.–4.
Person Responsible/Time:

Team 6-1
AGENDA
9:00 A.M.–9:30 A.M.

PERIOD | Items for Discussion
1-12 | ACTION
1 | Non-Negotiable Items

DATE:

TEAM MEETING AGENDA

MEMBERS PRESENT:

PERIODS ALLOTTED	TOPIC	DISCUSSION ACTION TAKEN WHAT IS TO BE DONE?	PRs AND TIMELINE WHO WILL DO IT? WHEN WILL IT BE DONE?

More Timesaving Ideas

Another timesaving strategy is to schedule any parent or student conferences at the end of the team meeting time. Decide how much time the conference will take and schedule that time block from the usual ending time for team meetings. If a parent or student is scheduled at the beginning of the team meeting time, be prepared for the conference to take up most, and usually all, of the team meeting.

Suppose the team meeting time is at 10:00 AM, and lasts 50 minutes. A parent wants to meet with the team. The team will schedule one team meeting period prior to the day of the parent meeting for planning. Planning should include: discussing when the parent is coming in, what the issues are, and who will facilitate the conference. (*In the chapter on parent contacts, I share how to plan for these parent meetings in detail.*) If the team decides to allow 20 minutes to meet with this parent, they will call the parent and schedule the conference for 10:25 AM. That way, the team will have 30 minutes to meet with the parent, and there is a natural ending time as the teachers have to get back to their classes. Notice that a 10:25 start gives the team a five-minute cushion.

Don't forget to leave the last period open whenever possible. Use this time not for coming to closure with unfinished topics, but rather to assign time at future meetings for unfinished topics. Also, team members can ask if there are new topics for upcoming meetings, and they can have a little time for a restroom break. It is important that the teachers give themselves a few minutes of cushion time between the end of the meeting and getting back to class.

Finally, the team should preassign certain topics to particular days of the week. For example, they may set aside the first three periods of every Wednesday to work on their curriculum map. That way, regardless of what else they may do on Wednesdays, they know that the first 15 minutes on Wednesdays will always be to work on curriculum. The team may plan for their advisory activities the first two periods on Fridays, determine how they are going to flex their schedule the first two periods on Thursdays, and work on their newsletter the first two periods on

Tuesdays. The rest of the time is open for any other things that come up. This way, teams insure that the ongoing things they need to address are scheduled, before they get bogged down in current issues.

Another bonus to having some topics prescheduled is that the support staff can plan to attend team meetings on certain days, in addition to the times they are invited to help with issues. For example, the administrator charged with curriculum development will always be at the team meeting on Wednesdays. There is no guessing what day the team is going to work on curriculum, because that is always the opening topic for Wednesday's meeting.

As an administrator, I remember that it was very helpful for the administrative team to know when teams were going to review discipline referrals. That way, my secretary could set up a weekly schedule for me and for the other administrators attending these team meetings. The same was true for my counselors. There are some meetings such as Thumbs Meetings that require an administrator and a counselor to participate. (These meetings are described in detail in the Positive Reinforcement and Student Management chapters.)

Teams should prioritize team topics that will be discussed and know how often the regular topics will be included on the agenda. Team members who know exactly what topics are going to start each team meeting are much more likely to come prepared. Team time is limited and very valuable, so teams need to be committed to getting the most out of every minute. On the following page is a sample weekly schedule for a team. The team begins each day with the topics listed and then proceeds with other items as needed.

Possible Weekly Team Schedule

Monday

- Positive calls home (one period)
- Set up parent meetings
- Use one period to plan for each parent meeting
- Calendar (one period)
- Activities for the week
- Homework and tests
- Reward strategies and celebrations (one period)
- Policy and procedure review (once a month for one period)

Tuesday

- Alternate Thumbs Up meetings with Pre-IEPs (four to six periods)
- Review every student by name in five criteria: academic performance, behavior, social, emotional, and personal
- Review team goals and adjust as needed the first Tuesday of each month (one or two periods)

Wednesday

- Curriculum Development (COWs) (three to four periods)
- Find and develop shared curriculum connections and assessments within the core team and the encore team
- Align curriculum with state standards and sample test items
- Service learning project
- Team newsletter (one period)

Thursday

- Flexing the schedule for next week (two to three periods) Changing class length, order, and student groupings
- Set up planning time for any upcoming events
- Follow-up Thumbs Up meetings (one period)
- Alternate professional development (three to four periods) and Team goal assessment (two to three periods)
- Develop strategies based on research and reading by team members (See Resources on page 239 for suggested books.)

Friday

- Finalize flexing schedule (one to two periods)
- Review discipline referrals (two to three periods)
- Advisory planning (two periods)

Each of the topics is discussed in detail in another chapter in this book. Notice that some of the topics are not on the agenda every week. In the sample schedule, the team alternates running Thumbs Up meetings with pre-IEPs on Tuesdays. That way, the team addresses each topic every other week, but always on Tuesdays. If teams coordinate their agendas, half of the teams in the building will be doing Thumbs Up meetings on the even weeks while the rest of the teams are running their pre-IEP meetings. Then they will all switch on the odd weeks. This way the administrators, counselors, and special needs staff can work with the appropriate teams.

It is important to include the time allotted for each topic on the agenda. Remember that one period is five minutes of team meeting time. Teams will find that topics require less time as they work regularly with them. The total amount of team meeting time available will be the biggest determining factor regarding the number of topics a team will be able to discuss and the amount of discussion time that will be available for each topic. The more rigorous a team is about setting time limits and adhering to the time limits, the more topics a team can complete.

Also notice that the time required for all of the prescheduled topics listed above takes up only a portion of the daily team meeting time. The time remaining is for day-to-day team management issues, parent meetings, and so on. *(Again, I always encourage teams to put the prescheduled topics at the beginning of the agenda. I have found that it is easier for teams to stick to the time limits for types of topics I have listed above.)* For example, if a team makes the team newsletter a weekly topic and uses one of the software programs available for creating newsletters, the task is easily accomplished. Rotate the responsibility for putting the newsletter together. Each team member should come ready to share something for the newsletter. Even with only one period a week, a newsletter can be sent out every few weeks.

If teams begin their team meetings with the day-to-day issues, they are less likely to get to the regularly scheduled topics. Teams have more difficulty putting time limits on the day-to-day student topics. That is why some teams struggle to get to topics like integrated curriculum and discipline referral reviews.

Roles and Responsibilities of Team Members

Assigning roles and responsibilities will help teams to function efficiently. Each role carries certain responsibilities, and the roles should be shared by the members of the team to maximize team performance. Every member should take on one or more of the roles listed below at some time. Members may rotate the roles yearly, or more often, but it is important that everyone on the team assume responsibility for how well the team functions by taking on a role or a combination of roles.

POSSIBLE ROLES and RESPONSIBILITIES of TEAM MEMBERS

TEAM LEADER/FACILITATOR
Facilitates team meetings and acts as the liaison for the team to the administration.

TIMEKEEPER
Keeps the time and enforces time limits established for each topic during team meetings.

SCRIBE/RECORDER/SECRETARY
Keeps the team notebook with the team agendas and notes from the meetings, contact logs, etc.

COMMUNICATOR
Asks the question "Who do we need to inform?" after each topic, and then gets the information out (like field-trip information to the exploratory teachers, cafeteria, and so on).

RESOURCE PERSON
Brings any materials needed like the curriculum map on curriculum development days, flip charts, certificates for Thumbs Meetings, and so on.

PUBLIC RELATIONS PERSON
This person works to promote team accomplishments with articles in the newspaper, a team newsletter, posting student work around town, and so on.

Teams may assign (*as needed*) other roles such as the team caller, the team member responsible for the team newsletter, or the team social director (*my favorite job!*).

The Team Contact Log

A team contact log can be of immense value to the team. In the team contact log, the team records all contacts made or attempted to parents, business partners, and others. Team members should consult the team contact log before making a contact. That way the team member knows how many times, or if at all, the parent has already been contacted. The team member may see that attempts before 5:00 PM have not been successful, and will know to call a little later in the evening.

The administrative team should also consult the team contact log before calling a parent, and they should also log all contacts they make in the teams' contact log. Many schools now have the capability to keep the contact logs electronically. Contact logs are successful when everyone logs all contacts, and everyone checks the calling log prior to making any contact.

Name: ____________________ Week of: ____________________

PHONE LOG

Date	Student	Parent/Guardian	Phone Conversation

Common Policies

Team members should begin the year by sharing classroom policies. It is important for teams to decide on as many common policies as possible. Most teachers have classroom rules regarding homework, paper headings, bathroom passes, grading and extra credit, and late assignments. Most teachers also create some sort of first-day information sheet they send home with their students. The teachers on the team need to share this information with each other.

After discussing the different issues, teachers on the team should come to consensus on team policies. This may, of course, be a difficult conversation when there are differences of opinion regarding policies. *(One of the biggest arguments I had to deal with between teachers was one team's discussion of their gum-chewing policy.)*

Early adolescents need consistency, and as the professionals, team members need to be able to agree on the policies. Then, expectations are the same as students go from class to class.

Coordinate Homework

Follow these three guidelines for homework assignments:

1) Homework should be assigned consistently.
2) Homework should be time-appropriate for the students' age.
3) Homework should be relevant.

A team can assure the first two stipulations if they work together to coordinate the homework.

Team members should share homework assignments daily and make sure that someone is assigning homework every night. The team also makes sure that the total amount of homework assigned will not take the students any more than about an hour.

So, teams work together to make sure that the students on a team have homework that is coordinated between the teachers. In the chapter on curriculum development, check out the idea that a single homework assignment can be graded by multiple teachers. This practice adds value and relevance to the work the students are doing.

TAG . . . You're It!

Getting the Most Out of the Workout!

Fitness Note: Doing the same exercise every time you work out will not result in maximum fitness benefits, and it will get boring. Instead you should work through a complete set of exercises over a period of time.

Apply this fitness concept to team meetings. Share the roles and responsibilities to help all of the team members grow. Establishing the topics for team meetings, and then setting the topics up on a regular rotation will ensure your team gets the most out the time you all put into team meetings.

Exercise One

If your team has established roles for all of the team members, try shifting roles for a few meetings until everyone has had the opportunity to try each of the roles. Then share and discuss what it was like in each of the roles. A list of possible roles is on page 30.

Exercise Two

If your team does not have roles and responsibilities assigned, then each team member should take one or more of the roles listed on page 32. Afterward, discuss how assigning roles impacted the mechanics of the team meeting.

Exercise Three

Practice using a timer as your team discusses a few topics. Estimate the number of periods that are needed and have the timekeeper use the timer and stop all discussion when time for a topic runs out. If time runs out before the discussion is finished, discuss why the time ran out. Did the team assign enough time? What could the team members have done to help finish the topic on time? How will the team apply this to future topics?

Exercise Four

Choose the "gottas" for your team meetings. Use the list of "gottas" on pages 22 and 23 to help you all get started. Prioritize the topics and determine how much time to put into each topic, and how often the topic should be addressed. Establish a team calendar and share that calendar with the administrative team and the rest of the teams in the school.

Interdisciplinary Curriculum Development

Getting Mentally Prepared: Developing Symphonic Curriculums

For any training to work, you have to be mentally prepared. The greatest coaches and personal trainers are also great teachers. They know that without a really good game plan they are not going to be successful. As legendary coach John Wooden said, "Failure to prepare is preparing to fail." Preparing an integrated approach to developing and delivering curriculum is like writing, practicing, and performing a symphony. When each of the instruments is played individually with perfection, it sounds very good; but when the individual instruments are played in unison with other instruments, the sound is incredible.

Like the individual instruments, each subject in the curriculum must be mastered and taught well. But like the musicians in a great symphony, the subjects must interact with each other to make the instruction more rigorous and relevant. Just like the instruments, the subjects do not always play at once. The impact of the music comes when each musician knows when to come in and when to let the others play. In integrated curriculums, the teachers know when to interact with other subject areas and when to continue on their own.

Good conductors know when the instruments enhance the sounds of other instruments, and when certain instruments should solo. In an integrated curriculum, the various subjects in a school are like the musical instruments. The teachers, as conductors, must know when a subject should stand alone, and when it should tie into other subjects.

So it was with the great composers. They wrote grand symphonies because they found natural connections between the various instruments and the music. They didn't try to force one part of the music to flow into another. The musical connection either happened naturally, or it didn't happen at all. The same is true of developing learning connections.

I am going to give you the format and the tools to create symphonic curriculums. I will demonstrate for you how to find where the connections between the various content areas of the curriculums happen naturally—to move beyond previous methods of integrating the curriculum into forced interdisciplinary units. Teachers today should never force connections by relating their subjects to an arbitrary theme.

Creating curriculum maps for the process of integrating curriculum is like creating musical scores. The process enables teachers to communicate with each other about what is going on in each of their classes, and results in the most integrated symphonic curriculums possible. As teachers work to find and develop real and relevant learning connections between subjects, they will also align each curriculum area with the state and national standards.

A learning connection is simply the opportunity created when any skills taught in one content area are also used in another content area.

I am going to share an easy-to-implement and very user-friendly process for teachers to find these opportunities and work together to expand and develop the skills that cross the curriculum areas. It is also exciting to see differentiated instruction develop as a natural by-product of this process.

Student performance on the high-stakes tests will improve as teachers learn to use this simple process to cross reference the standards between content areas. You will tie actual test items (released for practice) into the curriculum maps. Through the integration process, content area teachers in all areas, including related arts, will use the test items as a part of their instruction and assessments.

The curriculum maps also make it easier for schools to track and document how effectively programs such as technology and writing across the curriculum are being implemented, and how well common resources like the media center are being used. This process makes integrating the curriculum painless, and it also helps departments as they develop their individual curriculum areas.

In this book, these maps are called COWs, which stands for *Curriculum On the Wall.* This acronym came from a curriculum development workshop at which the curriculums were being displayed via overhead projector on a wall. Some of the

participants thought we needed a name for the maps and the process, and since the curriculum maps were on the walls, COWs seemed to be as appropriate as anything else. This acronym actually has nothing to do with the process, but it has stuck and is commonly used to refer to this particular method of curriculum mapping.

You will notice as you go through the rest of this chapter, many schools really play up the COW acronym and have a lot of fun with it! Although these maps are often displayed on the wall for curriculum development during the week, parent nights, business partnership meetings, and so forth, it is not necessary that they stay on permanent display. Most schools simply do not have the extra wall space to keep the maps displayed all the time.

Using this mapping process, we will quickly be able to identify the gaps in the tested curriculum areas where standards are not being addressed adequately or, in some cases, are even being ignored. We will also be able to easily identify duplication of the standards and to make decisions about curriculum compacting. Departments will actually do a quick item analysis for state test sample questions.

This process leads to a project-based curriculum and smoother transitions between grade levels. The power of the process is in the incredible levels of collaboration it creates between teachers, and the multi-layered approach it creates for ensuring student mastery of state and national standards.

The curriculum maps also encourage unprecedented levels of community involvement in the school. The maps foster programs such as COMPASS (COMmunity Partnerships Assuring Student Success), a partnership program with businesses and community groups that is based on curriculum topics demonstrated on the maps. The COWs are key to lifting curriculum collaboration to heights that were not previously considered. The steps in the curriculum mapping process and suggestions for using the COWs are outlined on the following pages.

Curriculum Mapping
Five Tasks for COWs

1. **Build the COWs by grade level**
   a. Teachers indicate what is taught in each subject area in a weekly outline format
   b. Build the maps by teams, if applicable
   c. Indicate state standards and test items on the maps
   d. Indicate media center use, technology implementation, writing programs, etc.

2. **Realign the instructional timelines and agree on curriculum as needed within departments**
   a. Teachers agree on common instruction and assessments
   b. Add sample state test questions to maps for documentation and use in instruction and assessments

3. **Find learning connections across curriculum areas**
   a. Look for topics that relate, and specific skills that will be used across curriculum areas

4. **Discuss and develop learning connections**
   a. Discuss, develop, and share reference points, activities, extra credit projects, PowerPoint slides, overheads, worksheets, assignments, and assessment items

5. **COMPASS—**
   Community Partnerships Assuring Student Success
   a. Develop a community-based curriculum
   b. Use the COWs as a communication tool to facilitate business partnerships that will help develop and support instruction

Build It and They Will Come

The first step in this process is building the maps. It is important to make the process as easy as possible. The maps can fit into the current planning process and remain very nonintrusive. Teachers already spend untold hours planning for their classes, so instead of adding to the workload, take advantage of the planning that has already taken place to get the

COW Tools

curriculum maps ready. Create a physically and visually interactive version of their curriculums. The curriculum maps should reflect in the simplest way possible what is currently being taught.

Teachers will be attaching adhesive notes, test items, and a variety of other notes to these boards at various times, so you should keep the COWs folded up in a poster board storage bin *(a barn?)* when not in use. The maps should be stored in a central area where they are easily accessible to everyone who might use them. Some schools have a room dedicated to the maps. Others will use team areas or departmental areas for the maps. The maps will not be useful if they are difficult to get to and use. These maps are to be used weekly and by multiple teachers and support personnel from different content areas. The idea is that the maps will be used indefinitely.

The pictures below show COWs in the early stages. *(I guess you could call these "calves.")* As you see, schools use various types of poster boards for this project. The basic materials needed are sturdy poster board and various sizes of adhesive notes.

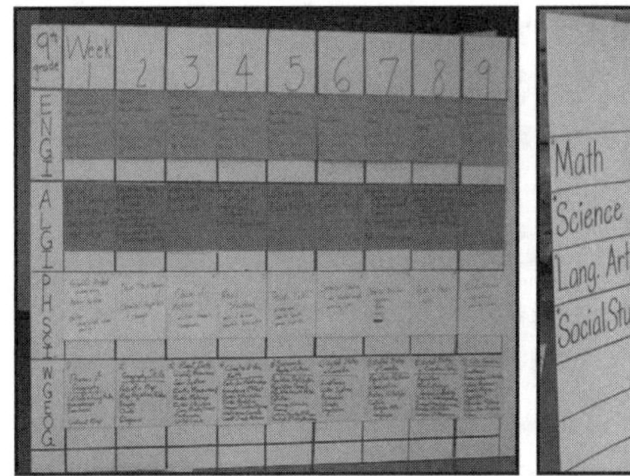

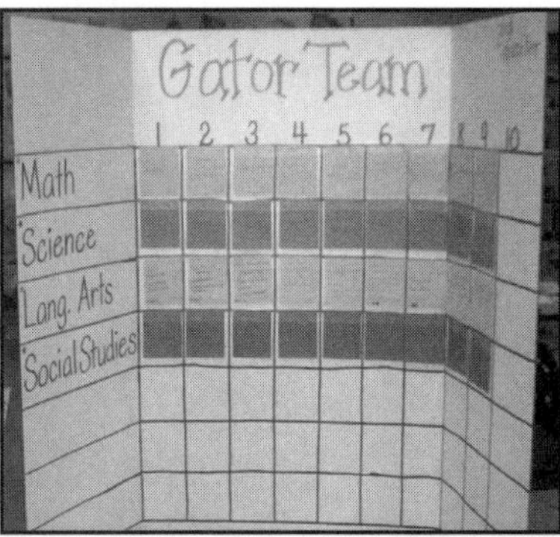

Schools use regular poster board or display boards for their maps.

On the poster boards, draw squares to correspond to the size of a regular adhesive note. Label the grid. List the subjects down the left side, and number weeks across the top. Each column will represent one week of curriculum in each subject area. Encourage teachers to use a different color adhesive note for each subject. For example, math might use blue notes, language arts might use yellow, social studies might use orange, and, of course, science could use green. Each elective/related arts/exploratory class should also have its own color.

Each adhesive note represents one week of curriculum in each area. Include three pieces of information on each adhesive note.

1) *The number of the week*
(If an adhesive note falls off, it will be easy to put it back in the correct spot.) The number of the week is not set in stone. Teams and schools build the

maps once, then adjust them as needed. If a teacher reaches a topic a couple of weeks earlier or later over the year, the map does not need to be changed.

2) *Content taught*
   Be as generic as possible when describing what is being taught. State the topic succinctly—the fewer words used, the better. (*A good tip: write large! Writing large on small piece of paper limits the amount that can be written. Also, the large print is so much easier to read.*) Do not include any description of instructional strategies or methodologies; give only an overall topic for what is taught. The more generic the title or topic, the more useful the map will be. If something is taught for several weeks, repeat the title as needed. For example, *Civil War* may be written in several weeks if needed.

3) *The state standard that is addressed by the week's topic*
   Most often, more than one standard is being taught, so all standards that might be covered by that topic should be listed. Use the numbers and letters that represent the standards, and do not write out the standards, as they are often quite lengthy.

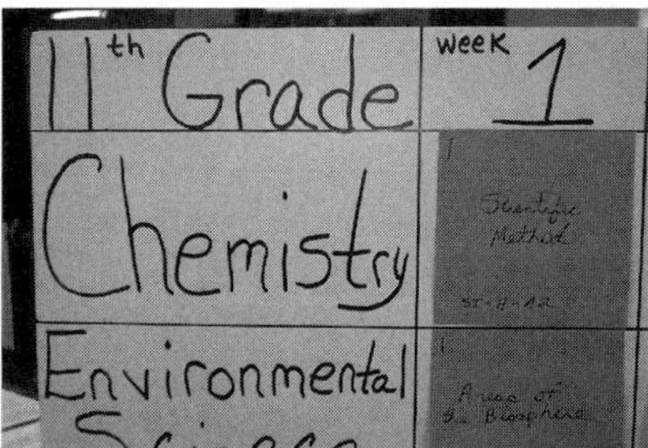

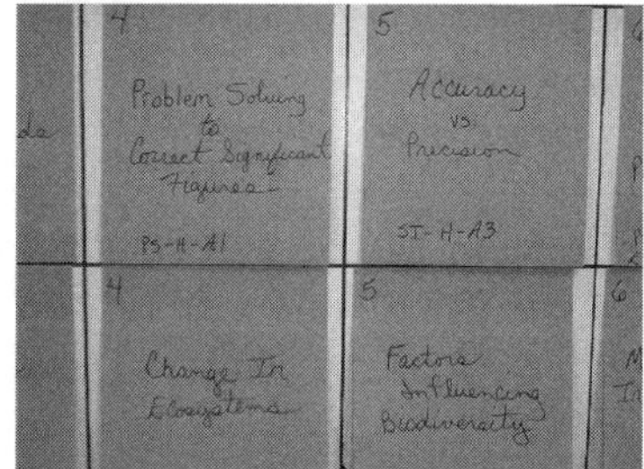

Middle school and high school examples of curriculum maps

Every team in the building should have its own map. This will allow each team to develop connections and units without being locked to another team. Once a month, the teams should share learning connections they are working on with the other teams at their grade level. While one team should not feel obligated to do a unit another team is doing, sharing is encouraged so that teams do not reinvent the same wheel over and over.

The elective team should create one curriculum map for each grade level. Each grade level elective curriculum map will show the elective classes available for that grade level. Most elective classes are available at each grade level. Even if some elective classes are really doing the same thing in more than one grade level, that elective teacher should duplicate the subject on each grade level map.

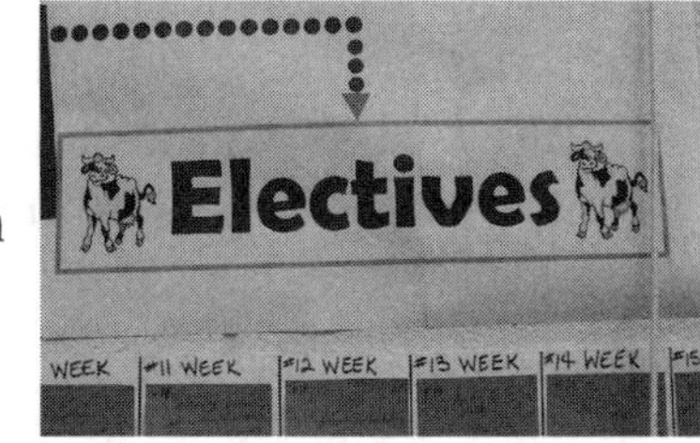

For example, sometimes there are cross-grade level elective classes, like band. Even though this band class is the same for two or more grade levels, it still should be written on each individual grade level curriculum map. Semester classes do not have to be written twice. Just number the weeks to indicate that the weeks are repeated in the second semester. So the square for Week 1 will be labeled Week 1 and Week 19, Week 2 becomes Week 2 and Week 20, and so on. This is an easy way to indicate that Week 1 in art repeats in Week 19 with new students.

Plan for the Future Using the Past

Teachers fill in the adhesive notes based on what they have done in the past. (*In curriculum workshops, I have teachers use last year's plan books and the district curriculum pacing guide to fill in the notes. We keep the task of building the maps easy because we want to build on the planning that has already been done.*) The maps show what is actually being taught in the current curriculums. Teachers and teams will work from there to plan for the future.

Ensuring Alignment With State Standards

After taking the high-stakes tests, students often come back and say things like "you didn't teach us some of that stuff." Of course, this is not what educators want to hear—especially since they worked so hard to make sure they addressed all of the standards in their area. However, a study of individual test items reveals the problem. Teachers may very well have covered the topic, but for some of the standards, they did not ask the kinds of questions that the state asks. The interpretation of the standard can vary, and often teacher-created test questions are worded differently than questions on the standardized tests.

So what teachers need to do is to accumulate all of the released and sample items for the state standards. The items are cut out so that individual test items are on separate strips of paper. By departments, teachers analyze each test item, read it aloud, and ask, "When would I ask this question?" Then the question is folded up and taped to the board under the appropriate week. The questions will fall into three categories:

1) **Questions that are currently in use**
   The department knows exactly where the state question fits into its curriculum, and that kind of question is often asked on current assessments. These questions are easily placed.

2) **Questions that assess skills that are taught, but are not being asked**
   The department agrees that these questions assess skills that are in its curriculum plan, but they are not being asked currently. This category also include questions the department knows should be on the board, but are difficult to place because they combine concepts, or have wording that might mislead students. These questions often confuse students.

3) **Questions that simply do not fit on the COWs**
   These questions assess topics or skills that are not currently in the curriculum. Sometimes teachers will argue that these items do not fit what they thought the corresponding state standard meant. Sometimes one grade level thinks another grade level is covering the topic, when actually it is not being covered by anyone. Needless to say, students generally do not perform very well on these test questions.

Every school I have worked with has had items that fall into all three categories when they look at the test items one at a time. This is why we ask teachers to look at each of the released test items and determine when that particular question would be asked. We very often hear, "I do not ask that particular question," or "I would not have asked that question in that way." Every teacher-constructed test should not look just like the state test by any means, but every state question should be a part of the instruction and assessment process the teachers will use for each unit of instruction.

After the teachers have placed the state sample assessment items on the curriculum maps, they will make copies of the assessment items for each instructional unit. These assessment items along with the ones already developed for the unit are an important part of the planning for each instructional unit.

This is a very visual process, and if there happen to be any gaps in the curriculums, they are easy to see. Weeks where there are no test items attached to the map indicate that what is being taught those weeks is not assessed by the state proficiency tests. That does not mean the content in those areas is not important, or that it should not be taught. However, if there are several weeks in any content area where there are no released questions attached, the department should purposefully look at that content and determine what its curriculum priorities are going to be.

The departments may want to reduce the amount of time spent on areas that are not tested, and put some effort into the "category two questions" (those that are confusing), and the "category three questions" (those that are not being covered at all).

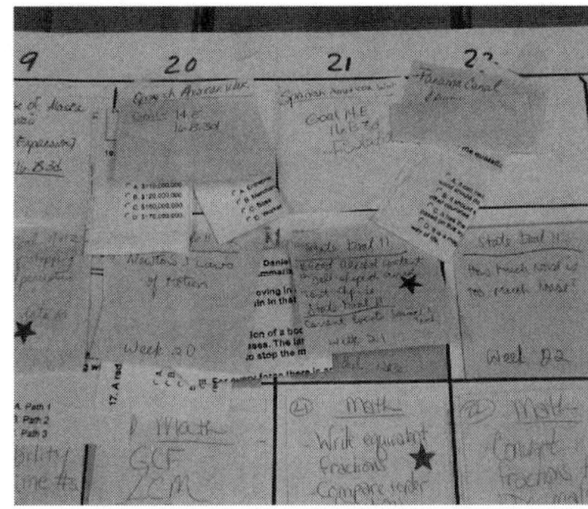

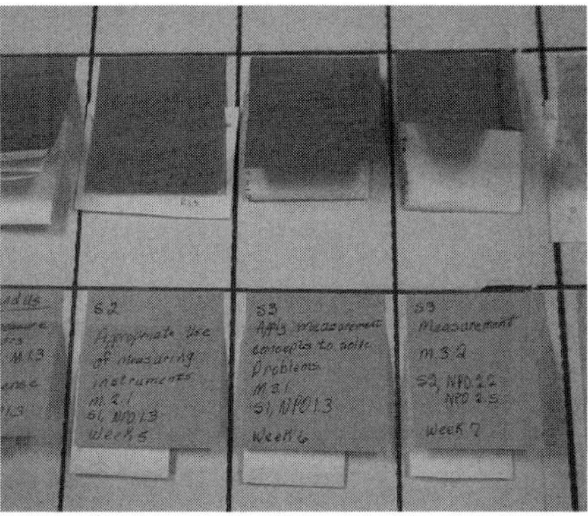

Seeing Dots—Exploratory Classes, Programs, and Educational Resources

The curriculum maps can track information in other important areas, too. For example, use small sticky dots (available at office supply stores) to track the use of technology and the media center. In one school, the teachers use blue sticky dots to indicate the use of technology in their classes. First, determine what the use of technology includes. (*Showing videos doesn't count.*) Then each teacher simply puts a blue dot on any week where he or she uses technology as a part of their instruction and assessment.

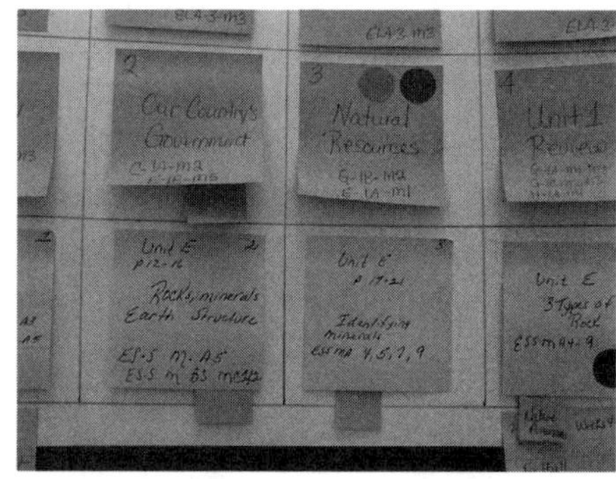

The technology experts for the school or district can look at the maps and quickly see where technology is already being utilized successfully. They can then provide support for teachers more effectively and efficiently. For example, as new software applications become available, they know where it can best be used. They can schedule computer time more efficiently. Technology coordinators will see the gaps in the use of technology within the building. If there are no blue dots in a content area, the coordinators can help teachers apply technology. The COWs also show which staff members might need assistance with training or the implementation of technology.

The same school asked teachers to put a red dot in any week where they used the media center as a part of their instruction. Again, they had to discuss what they were going to consider as the actual use of the media center. For example, they decided that teachers occasionally letting students go to the media center to return books would not be considered using the media center as part of instruction. There were several teams that did not have a single red dot on their subject row.

With this visual process, anyone can tell at a glance what colors are included in what rows, and of course, what colors are missing in some subjects. That gives the media specialists much needed information, and allows them to be much more proactive and productive. Media specialists can look at the COWs, identify places where there is limited use, look at the topics, and make specific suggestions to those teachers for the use of the media center. The media specialists will be able to plan well in advance of impending projects.

Dots and curriculum maps can help build a school's community partnership program. Share the maps with various businesses and community groups. Ask them to indicate with a star, dot, or note any topics that fit into their area of expertise. (For detailed information on possible partnerships, review Chapter Four—COMPASS, which stands for Community Partnerships Assuring Student Success.)

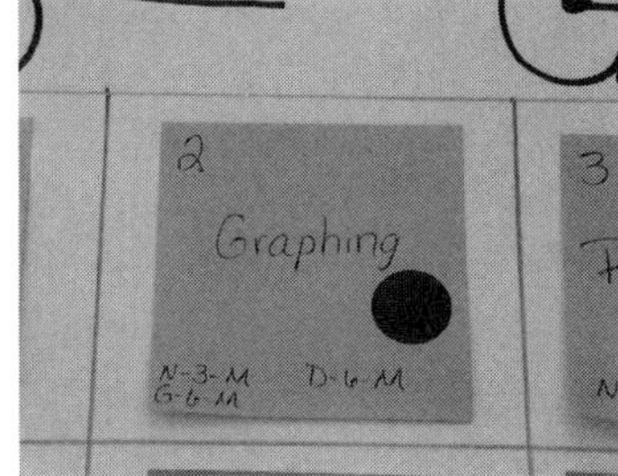

Connecting The Dots—Finding Learning Connections

Ask teachers to review the maps for a few minutes every week. On a weekly basis, teachers should be using the maps either to find a new learning connection, or to be discussing and developing learning connections they have found. The team should make curriculum development a prescheduled weekly team-meeting topic. First, ask teachers to look at any row other than their own. As they look at another curriculum area, they are to look for a key word or phrase that would match a skill they teach in their own area.

LEARNING CONNECTIONS—any time a teacher finds that a skill taught in his or her content area is also used in another content area. When teachers identify *learning connections,* then they work together to develop and demonstrate the application of the skill in both areas.

For example, the math teacher might look for places where charts and graphs are used in other subject areas. This could lead to a discussion with the social studies teacher. Together the two teachers look at how charts and graphs are used in the social studies unit on elections. In fact, the math teacher will undoubtedly find numerous places where charts and graphs are used in various core classes and encore classes.

Since there will often be multiple learning connections for any skill, it is not surprising that a skill is taught and applied at different times. Most learning connections happen over an extended time. It is a misconception that interdisciplinary instruction means everyone must work on the same "theme" or teach the same skill at the same time. Teachers should not have to change the order and timing of their subject to coincide with another teacher, if it does not fit the natural flow of their subject.

The language arts teacher might look for topics from other areas when beginning a unit on descriptive paragraphs. The teacher might give students suggested topics for their descriptive paragraphs that are drawn from things they have already studied in other classes (polygons, molecules). Or the teacher might begin the k (I already know) part of a k–w–l chart for one of the other teachers by having students describe what they already know about something they are going to be studying later. The science teacher might look for applications of the scientific method in other subject areas.

When one teacher sees a topic in another area that requires the same skill he or she teaches, the skill should be marked on the COW. The teacher creates an adhesive note of a new color. (This note can be a full size or one of the small index tabs.) The teacher writes the skill he or she teaches, the week, and the state standards associated with the skill on the new note, and attaches the note to the other subject area's row in the place where the connection could occur. The note is placed under the original note to signal the possible connection. Any time teachers see notes attached underneath the original notes, they know that another teacher is indicating that there may be a learning connection between two curriculum areas.

Developing Learning Connections

Basically the maps become big notepads on which teachers can write notes to one another indicating an interest in common topics. Once teachers have found learning connections, the next task is to discuss and develop them. Here is a list of some possibilities for developing learning connections.

Developing Learning Connections

When developing learning connections, teachers should consider different levels of connections. (Details for each level are described on pages 47–57.)

1. **Refer to the use of the same skill in both classes.**
   Teachers connect skills in one class to specific topics and times in other classes. So a teacher tells students specifically when and where the skills they are learning will be used in other classes.

2. **Share demonstration materials.**
   Teachers share resources that are appropriate in both classes (overheads, PowerPoint slides, supplemental resources).

3. **Share instructional activities.**
   Teachers use the same worksheets in both classes. Students complete part of the worksheet in one class and the remainder of the worksheet in another class.

4. **Give students guided choice assignments.**
   For example, the language arts teacher gives students writing choices with the topics selected from content in other classes.

5. **Give students extra credit for the work done in another teacher's class.**
   The value and relevancy of work goes up for students when they receive credit for the work from more than one teacher.

6. **Share assessment items.**
   Assessment items from each area should show up on multiple assessments in multiple content areas.

7. **Save and share student work to develop embedded themes and ongoing projects.**
   Combinations of learning connections will lead to recurring embedded themes and ongoing projects. Saving student work will require the teachers to assist students in maintaining portfolios.

First, a Note About Timing—Timing Is Everything!

Learning connections may happen concurrently. Teachers may be able to develop and implement the learning connection and coordinate activities at the same time. For example, the language arts teacher may teach how to use the internet for research, at the same time the social studies teacher is having students investigate a famous black American for Black History Month. So the two teachers work together on the project, and the students get two grades on the one project—one for language arts and one for social studies.

Many teachers consider only concurrent connections when they are thinking about learning connections. It is important to note that only occasionally will the timing of skills being taught in one content area line up nicely with what is happening in another content area. Because of that, teachers may feel they need to change the sequence of their lessons to align with the content of the other area, whether it fits the flow of their class or not. Or, even worse, all of the teachers on the team are told that they have to tie their subjects into one theme all at the same time, regardless of whether or not it is timely for their subject. *(This should never happen.)*

A teacher should never be forced to adapt his or her curriculum to another teacher's curriculum if it does not naturally fit with the flow of the class at the time. *(Later in this chapter, I will demonstrate how to develop themes in the more appropriate, natural way.)*
It is much more likely that learning connections will happen over extended periods of time. If we do not limit ourselves to concurrent learning connections, the number of learning connections is unlimited.

Imagine learning connections that happen over an extended period of time. Although a skill taught in one area may not be used in another area for weeks or even months, the skill will probably be used in multiple areas many times throughout the year. The number of possibilities for these extended learning connections is endless. One teacher can be referencing something in another teacher's class that is not going to happen for many weeks or even months. (The learning connections become *distributed practice*.)

When teachers look for learning connections that happen over an extended period of time, they can also begin to develop ongoing projects that grow throughout the school year. Students develop portfolios to hold developing projects that require different work from each of the subject areas during the year. Interdisciplinary units (IDUs) are powerful and motivating for students, but it's a terrible waste to develop only connections that happen in the same week or two in a traditional interdisciplinary unit.

For example, the math teacher may see that the social studies teacher teaches a unit on elections, and the math teacher is about to teach a unit on charts and graphs. The problem is that the social studies teacher does not teach the elections unit until weeks 28–30, and the math teacher plans to teach charts and graphs in weeks 8–10. It is important that both teachers teach their content in the appropriate sequence. Do not ask the social studies teacher to move the unit to weeks 8–10 to match the math sequence, but create a powerful connection anyway.

During the team meeting designated for curriculum development, the math teacher should ask the social studies teacher if charts and graphs are important to the elections unit. The social studies teacher gives the math teacher examples of charts and graphs from the social studies book, along with worksheets and assessments used during an elections unit in the social studies class. *(Electronic files are particularly helpful!)*

The math teacher copies the materials. Then the math teacher does a little "cutting and pasting" and has new worksheets to use with the charts and graphs unit. The students are blown away by the fact that each one of the examples on the new worksheets comes directly from their social studies book and class materials.

Reference One Class in Another

Often students ask, "When are we ever going to use this stuff again?" Now the math teacher can say, "In twenty weeks and two days, you will use these very same problems in the social studies class." The math teacher can even reference the chapter and page numbers in the social studies book. In addition, the social studies teacher might suggest that the math teacher put an opinion question on each of the worksheets to get student opinions and knowledge about the election process. The students get credit in math for giving their opinions about elections, while the social studies teacher gets valuable information to use for planning for the elections unit later in the year.

Share Instructional Materials and Activities with Other Teachers

When the math teacher finishes the unit, the completed worksheets are given to the social studies teacher to hold until the elections unit. During the elections unit, the social studies teacher will have the students use their math work to help them complete their social studies assignments. The students think it is great to already have some of the answers, and the teachers know it is great to have the students revisiting the math work. The social studies teacher asks students to revise their responses to the opinion questions as they go through the elections unit. *(Often students do not like to be involved with revisions; however, these revisions are different because the original assignment is for another teacher.)*

Another example of a learning connection is developed between the art teacher and the math teacher. The art teacher notices the phrase "line design" in the math teacher's row. The art teacher attaches a note with the words "string art" on it. The math teacher has no clue what string art is. When the art teacher and the math teacher meet, the math teacher learns that string art is a physical representation of a line design created on boards using nails or pegs and a variety of textures of string such as fishing line and yarn. Now the math teacher uses the string art as a portion of the assessment rubric for his unit on line design. All math students rotate through the art class during the school year. As the math students rotate through the art class, the math teacher will give the students points for completed string art projects done in art class. The art teacher uses the line designs generated in math as the templates for students to use in art, and the art and math grades become interdependent.

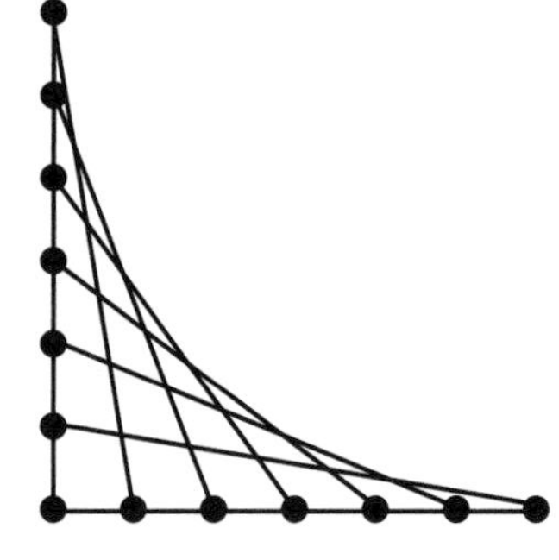

State standards are involved in each of the examples. The social studies teacher references sample questions to see how questions for charts and graphs will look on the math portion of the state test. The math teacher will have examples of social studies questions, and the two teachers will reinforce each other's curriculum. The math teacher can share with the art teacher the types of questions asked regarding angle classification and measurement, and specifically how they are worded. When all teachers share their assessments, students see some of the same assessment items on multiple assessments in multiple areas.

Offer Guided Choice Assignments and Extra Credit

Guided choice assignments are powerful because students feel more ownership since they have some choice in the work they do. For example, the language arts teacher has been teaching the students about descriptive writing and is ready to have the students actually do some writing for evaluation.

The language arts teacher gives the students several choices developed from the COWs and team planning. The students may choose to write descriptive paragraphs about topics such as molecules, polygons, biomes, the Internet, sculpture, and music composition. The language arts teacher includes two possibilities from each of the subjects that the students are taking.

The writing task and the skills are the same regardless of the topic chosen, and yet, the students will report every time that they are going to write about the "easy" one. Of course, learning preferences play a big role in the students' choices, and a student's interest level in the writing improves with the element of choice. Guided choices provide relevancy to both subjects involved.

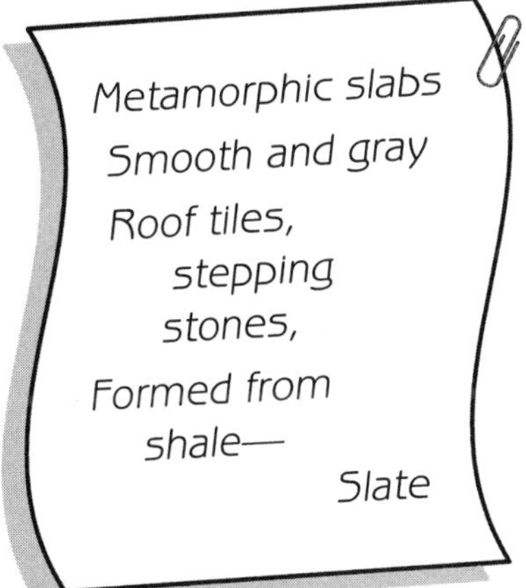

Metamorphic slabs
Smooth and gray
Roof tiles,
stepping
stones,
Formed from
shale—
Slate

Students will also become more invested in the assignment if extra credit is available. The team may decide that any time a student participates in work in one class that relates to another, the second teacher will give the student extra credit. To receive credit, students show the completed assignment to the second teacher. The assignment now carries grade value in two classes. Two teachers are encouraging students to complete the assignment, and to do it well.

Learning Connections Become Embedded Themes, Ongoing Projects, and Often Yearlong Projects

One social studies teacher developed a learning connection with a science teacher. They connected the local history of their area and an environmental unit. Since logging was a major part of the local history, the social studies teacher recognized a natural connection with the study of the rainforest that was a part of a science environmental unit. The science teacher taught the environmental unit a few months before the social studies teacher introduced the local history. The social studies teacher required students to compare and contrast what is happening to the rainforest today with how logging evolved in their area, in the United States, and around the world.

In science, the students visited previously logged sites to see the environmental impact, and to view the reforestation process. The students also visited a museum and sawmill to see how the logging industry evolved and to observe its impact. Several pieces of work from the environmental unit provided a starting point for work in the history unit. The two teachers gave the students extra credit for each piece of science that related to social studies, and vice versa.

Meanwhile, within the same team, the language arts teacher developed a learning connection with the math teacher. The math teacher put students in five-person "construction companies" and gave students the directions for building three different decks. (She got the plans from a local lumberyard.) Students were given this scenario:

> *A new subdivision is being built with several hundred new homes. Each home will include one of the three decks. Your construction company would like to build all of the decks. Prepare a bid for the job, giving a detailed line-item cost analysis.*

The language arts teacher saw a potential learning connection. During a unit on business letter writing, students could write a cover letter for the bid. The math teacher taught the bid unit first, and saved the student work. Several weeks later, the language arts teacher took the bids, and helped students organize the information and write professional cover letters.

A Real World Connection

One year, during this unit, the science teacher was actually building a deck at his home, which was located a few blocks from the school. Several of the bus routes passed near the science teacher's home, and the students started pressing the science teacher for information about his deck to try to get the inside track on their bids. One of the student teams asked to visit the project at the science teacher's house. The science teacher agreed to let the students visit, and was proud to show his handiwork and answer their questions. Two of the girls in the groups were looking at his directions and some of the boards he had precut to show the students, and they were happy to let him know that he had cut them incorrectly according to the schematic he was working from. The embarrassed science teacher quickly replied, "I meant to do it that way." Improvising, he said, "See that small oak tree? As you can see, the deck is going to go past the oak tree, so I have cut these boards shorter to allow room for the tree. It is a small oak tree now, but I want to have room when it grows."

Hearing this, one of the boys in the group asked, "Why don't you just cut down the oak tree?" Like any good steward of the environment, the science teacher was worried about this response and asked why the students would even consider such a thing.

Another student replied, "You see, we're businessmen now. Our company is going to buy the materials, precut them, and store them by design. All we have to do is pick up the materials, go to the site, and put the deck together. If we were to have to change the design, it would take more time and then cost us more. When you own your own company, time is money!"

Needless to say, the science teacher was not impressed with time and money taking priority over the environment. So he asked the students, "What is your company's environmental policy?" The students said, quite matter-of-factly, that an environmental policy was not part of the assignment. They just had to determine how much they were going to charge to build each of the decks. *(Given the nature of this chapter, I am sure you already know what happened next.)* The science teacher was not going to let this go on, and another project was born.

A project which began in math with an interesting assignment to bid on an imagined construction project moved numerous times through the language arts curriculum. The science teacher added the task of writing an environmental policy. The students became environmental specialists for their construction companies. They had to determine what the environmental issues might be with construction projects. For practice, they did an environmental impact study of the school to determine where decks might be best added for outside activities at the school. The students saved their policies in portfolios with their previous work.

Portfolio Records

Interdisciplinary projects require the development of portfolio records. In the construction company scenario, students worked with the language arts teachers and their advisors throughout the year to manage their portfolios. Language arts teachers helped students with the technical aspects of putting together a professional-looking project. Advisors helped students physically manage their portfolios by making sure the students put the appropriate various pieces of work into them. The portfolios were kept in the advisors' rooms. All teachers are advisors, so they helped all of the students with their subject part of the project, and each teacher worked with his or her advisory group to maintain the portfolios. The teachers and students worked together to turn the separate pieces of work into a consolidated project. Here's what it looked like:

First, the math teacher put the students into their construction companies and they worked on the itemized bids. Later, the language arts teacher had the students add a cover letter, format their bids, and put it all in a presentation folder. In science class, the students considered possible environmental issues as they determined the costs for building the decks. A little later the students studied the local history, and the social studies teacher had the students write a fictitious history of their construction company based on the real history of the area. Along the way, the students crafted numerous revisions, with the appropriate teachers giving the students extra credit and signing off on the project again.

Students documented mastery of skills when they added examples of their work to their portfolios. The portfolio elements were not just random examples of work, but rather a combination that became an impressive project. The language arts teacher was able to reference the different styles of writing the students used when working on the various parts of the project to document mastery of several writing standards.

For example, when students worked on the revisions of the history of their construction companies, they were polishing their narrative writing skills.

The elective teachers are integral in establishing learning connections. In fact, as most interdisciplinary projects develop, the elective teachers play the central roles.

It has been my experience that as this process goes forward, many of the projects actually originate in the elective classes. So it is critical that the elective teachers work on the curriculum maps weekly, as they will find the students are applying many of the core skills in their classes.

In the deck project, the language arts teacher and math teacher work with the technology teacher to teach the students about spreadsheets and publishing. As the students cycle through the exploratory classes, the industrial tech teacher helps the students build scale models of their decks for display, the business teacher works with the students on marketing, and the media specialist helps the students put together multimedia bid presentations. The students add to their project at different times in different exploratory classes throughout the year. *(Notice the important collaboration between the core and the exploratory teachers.)*

Near the end of the school year, the student construction companies produce bid presentations for school board and community members. By the time students make their bid presentations, they have an impressive product to share. Each student will have published a binder with the cover letter, a bid created on spreadsheets, their company's environmental policy, and a history of their company. They will have scale models of the decks and, as a company, will make a multimedia bid presentation.

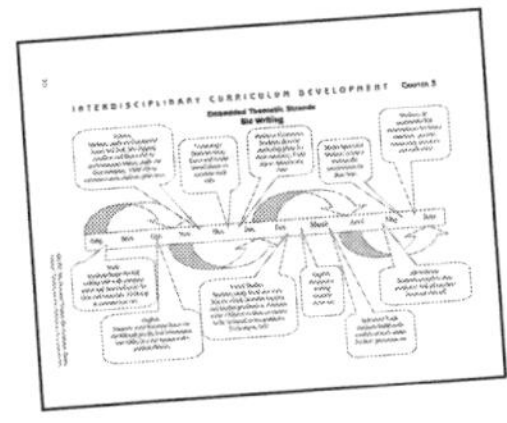

I have included on page 70 a graphic demonstrating the organization of this project. Note how the skills and topics spiral and thread through the school year.

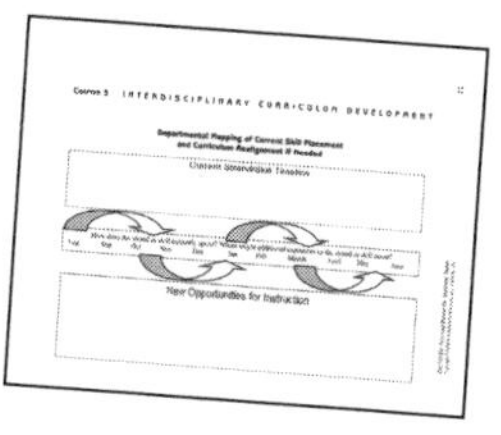

There is a blank form on page 71 for departments to use to show where skills are currently taught and where they might be expanded.

On page 72 is a blank form for any team to use to develop interdisciplinary skills use across the content areas.

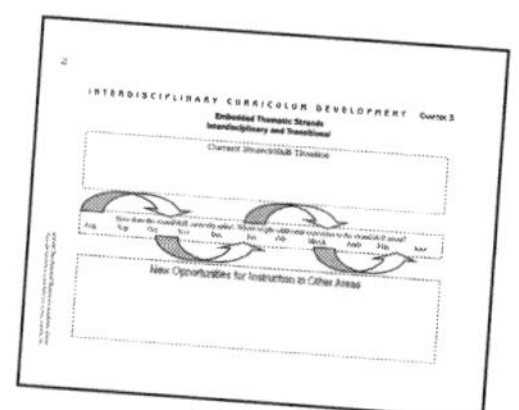

On page 73 are examples of how teachers have used this form.

On pages 66 and 68 are two different planning charts. Reproduce one of these or create one of your own to plan for interdisciplinary curriculum projects.

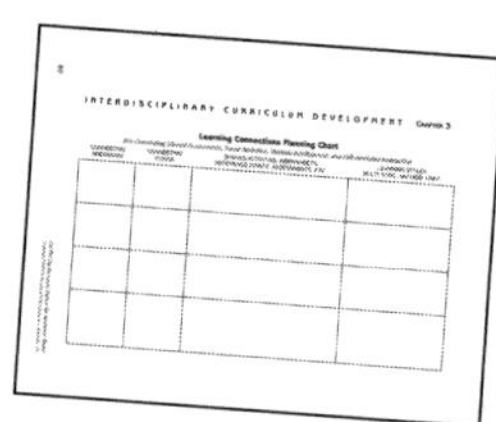

Examples of the ways actual academic teams used the charts are included on pages 67 and 69.

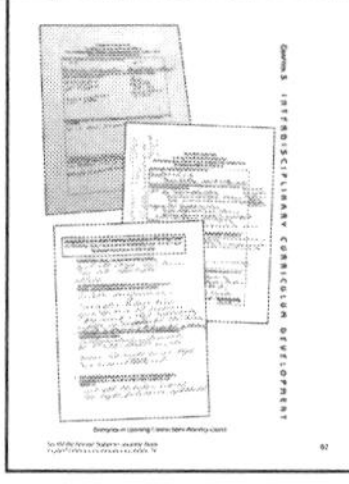

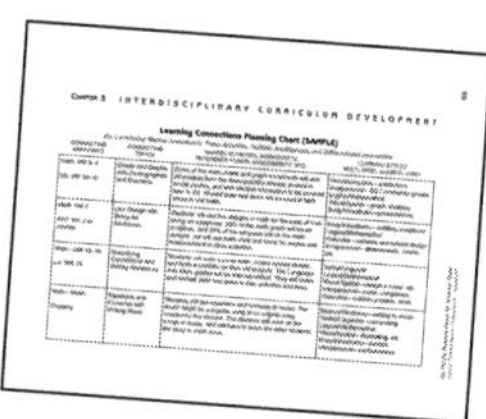

The Transient Student

More Advantages for Project-Based Learning

What happens to the student that moves in sometime during the year and comes into the project somewhere in the middle? Students moving in and out of schools during the year have always been an issue, and in some areas a very large issue. This is another reason for yearlong projects. These projects make it easier to bring new students up to speed when they move into a class.

When a student moves in, he or she is given copies of the work completed thus far for the project. The project puts the classwork into the context of the team project. The new student adds new work to the project along with other students. One bonus is that the new student becomes part of a "construction company" and has several students to collaborate with from the very first day in class.

Remember that all of the core teachers and many of the exploratory teachers are using the yearlong project. Since the project is interdisciplinary and therefore crosses several curriculum areas, the new student has a common thread to help him or her get to know all of the teachers. That means the student can ask for help on this one project in the technology class, the math class, the English class, the art class, the science class, and . . . *(You get the idea!)*.

Many teachers and teams I work with are in highly transient areas such as locations where migrant families live and work. As these teachers work with the COWs and develop cross-curriculum, ongoing projects, they report the learning connections and interdisciplinary projects help them bring new students up to speed. Some students will leave school at some time during the year, and come back again as their parents move for work. It is nice for these students to be a part of the project before they leave, and then get their own portfolios back again when they return.

Shared Assessment Items

As an interdisciplinary project develops during the year, each teacher passes on the assessment they have used. The subsequent teachers will use assessment items from previous assessments, as is appropriate, in their classes. Sometimes, the assessment items need a little tweaking, but most often they can be used verbatim. It is easy to tag those assessment items to demonstrate to the students when and where they had previously had that very same assessment item.

As teachers find and develop other learning connections, the students will participate in many projects during the school year. Each of the projects is started by finding learning connections where skills from one area can be used in another area. All projects are developed from combinations of learning connections, and each project is always built upon required skills.

Since the state test items for the skills are attached to the curriculum maps, the teachers will use those questions as a part of the instruction and assessment that is being developed and shared between content areas. So, some of the shared assessment items are also state test items. Just imagine the items showing up multiple times in multiple content areas, and yet always in context.

Remember, this includes the related arts classes as well. (And just when you thought that it could not possibly get any better, we begin to develop common assessments!)

On occasion these learning connections happen in such a way that they become an interdisciplinary teaching unit (IDU). The only difference between the deck project described and a traditional IDU is the timing. The learning connections in the deck project did not happen simultaneously. In an IDU, learning connections are done simultaneously in a given time period. Let the natural timing of the learning connections determine how they are designed (more about IDUs later).

Coordinating Curriculum with Special Programs such as "Magnet Programs," etc.

The COWs are also incredibly helpful in threading magnet strands through core classes. A school may have three magnet programs like business, engineering, and health/medical. Students' exploratory classes for the most part will be in those fields. Sometimes teams are set up according to the academies, but it is much more likely that teachers teach math, English, history, or science and have students from two or even all three programs on their team and in the same class at the same time. So, the question becomes how to design classes with connections to all of these magnet programs. If one teacher had to independently plan a variety of experiences targeted toward the different strands, it would be a huge task, and very time consuming.

The COWs provide a quick reference guide for core teachers to reference examples of topics and activities from different elective/related arts/exploratory programs that are easily incorporated into their classes, and vice versa. Teachers can ask the exploratory teachers to share assignments, activities, and assessments that relate to their core subject. The core teachers can then begin to create assignments and activities relevant to what different students will experience in their specific programs. The core teachers share the state standards and corresponding assessment items which, in turn, become part of the elective/related arts/exploratory assessments.

Most magnet programs are driven by the exploratory classes, so the exploratory teachers should be working with the COWs every week, looking at the core subjects and offering suggestions to the core teachers. This way, the core teachers are able to offer "guided choice" assignments based on the magnet strands and the suggestions of the magnet teachers.

The language arts teacher may give students a choice of three different topics for their narrative paragraphs based on experiences that have already happened in the three magnet strands. This helps maintain the integrity and identity of the various academies within a single class.

The exploratory teachers have the examples and activities, so by using the COWs teachers save planning time. Of course, the core classes are built around the state standards for each area, which means as students participate in interdisciplinary projects, they will be addressing the state standards and assessment examples in the exploratory and magnet classes. In this way, the state standards are cross-referenced between the exploratory and core subjects, as well as among the core subjects. *(This means your school will continually improve student performance on those pesky state tests!)*

Differentiate Instruction Naturally

With each learning connection, teachers naturally differentiate their instruction. Different subjects naturally appeal to different learning styles and intelligences. By bringing other subjects into a class, teachers appeal to different learning styles and intelligences. Consider the following chart which shows some of the learning connections one math teacher found.

Differentiating Math Through Learning Connections

Subject Areas	*Topics*
■ Math—Art	Line Design
■ Math—Science	Graph Data
■ Math—Life Skills	Exponents
■ Math—Social Studies	Projections
■ Math—P.E.	Personal Graphs
■ Math—Language Arts	Write Expressions
■ Math—Technology	Spreadsheets
■ Math—Music	Fractions
■ Math—Business	Percents
■ Math—Shop	Scale Models
■ Math—Vocal Music	Raps/Songs for Formulas

This list is only a beginning. With each learning connection, another teacher in the building helps the math teacher with examples and activities. As a result, other teachers have thus helped the math teacher incorporate the multiple intelligences and all the learning modalities.

I have developed several forms to help teachers plan and document learning connections. Teachers record which subjects are involved in the learning connection and the expected timelines. Then the teachers indicate shared activities. They also document the multiple intelligences addressed by each teacher in the learning connection. There is a vertical learning connection planning chart on page 66 and examples of completed charts on page 67. There is a horizontal learning connection planning chart on page 68 and completed examples on page 69.

As teachers struggle to differentiate instruction and meet the needs of the widely diverse student populations, it is important that they find an easy way to share strategies. Teachers have always shared and developed instructional strategies within their various departments. The teachers in each department have worked to ensure that the state standards are being met and students receive quality instruction. It is imperative that teachers share strategies, activities, and assessments across departmental lines. Cross-referencing strategies, activities, and assessments between departments is the only way to further improve on the quality departmental work that has been done. Using an integrated approach to develop curriculum guarantees that differentiated instruction is going to happen naturally. It also guarantees that the learning experience becomes more relevant for the student. Finally, the state standards are automatically cross-referenced and repeated in multiple subject areas. That means students will perform better on the high-stakes state assessments.

"Old School" Interdisciplinary Teaching Units

It is a popular misconception that integrating curriculum means that all of the teachers on the team should be involved with the same topic at the same time. This is often referred to as the Interdisciplinary Teaching Unit (IDU), or Thematic Teaching Unit. Getting two teachers to line up their curriculums occasionally is difficult enough. It takes a tremendous amount of collaboration and practice *(not to mention the perfect alignment of the planets)* to pull off an effective interdisciplinary unit.

Most often, the teachers pick a central theme, then work to try to fit their curriculums into the theme. While doing this they often work in isolation. For example, the teachers work together to decide what theme might best fit their subjects, what the time frame will be, and hopefully, what sort of closing activity they might plan. After that, the teachers often work on their own *(quite hard, I might add)* to develop lessons for each subject area that will relate to the theme.

The teachers often fill out some sort of form to indicate what they will be doing in each subject area related to the theme. They usually indicate what GLEs (Grade Level Expectations) will be met during the unit. So let's say that the team decides to develop an "Egyptian" thematic unit. The math teacher will work to redesign lessons or create new lessons to relate the math skills to the Egyptian theme. The science, social studies, language arts, and some related arts teachers will all redesign or create new lessons for the Egyptian unit.

It has been my experience that art teachers receive the most requests to do things for core areas that do relate to what the art curriculum says the art teachers should be doing at any one time.

Since the theme is used in all of the classes for the length of the IDU, students will see how each class can be related to the central theme, but not necessarily to other classes and disciplines. This is particularly evident in classes where the natural flow has been changed to relate to the theme. There are some great math lessons that relate to the pyramids, but the math teacher may not have been ready to teach those math concepts. Sometimes this situation feels forced, and teachers say things like "I had to stop teaching my regular curriculum to participate in the IDU."

Before starting an IDU, every teacher has to ask the same questions.

- What skills might be used in the study of Egypt?
- Are those skills taught in this course?
- Do the skills correspond to state standards to be taught?
- Are the skills new or a review of previously learned skills?
- Do the skills fit into the flow of the class, or will I have to stop my teaching plan to fit into the Egyptian unit?

Teachers work very hard to relate each of their subjects to the theme, but not always to each other's subjects. Instead of taking advantage of the planning process, the teachers' workload is increased, which often leads to more frustration than productivity. Teachers are much more likely to participate in developing ongoing interdisciplinary learning connections if they never have to change the flow and sequence of their subjects.

Remember, build learning connections one at a time, and projects and units will emerge with the essential questions already answered and most of the work already done. Shared skills should be the driving force in learning connections—not just a theme.

Pretty quickly sets of learning connections connect to other sets of learning connections, which means four or more teachers are automatically involved.

As ongoing projects emerge naturally from the learning connections, themes begin to evolve from the projects. Since the learning connections are built on shared skills first, the projects and interdisciplinary units that evolve support skills and the state standards. Instead of picking a theme and trying to match skills to the theme, the skill connections came first, and then projects and themes emerged.

Interdisciplinary instruction is not about connecting classes to some theme. Interdisciplinary instruction is about connecting classes through common skills.

Don't Force Thematic Units

The number of potential learning connections is virtually endless. As teachers practice developing learning connections, they begin to see how their subject might better fit with some of the others. Naturally, some of these learning connections will actually happen concurrently between the subjects. That means that occasionally the teachers will find that multiple learning connections may come together nearly simultaneously and they will have everyone working on a learning project at the same time. Then a learning project becomes a "thematic unit," or IDU. *(Simply give it a name such as "the rainforest unit" or "the national parks unit." Everything else has already been done.)*

Documenting the Learning Connections

Teachers need to document learning connections as they develop them. Use the forms on pages 66 and 68 or develop similar ones. This record is especially helpful for new teachers coming into the team. By looking at learning connections the previous teachers developed, the new teacher has a point of reference, and the "connecting" teachers are automatically invested in the new teacher. The new teacher and current teachers have a foundation on which to build.

These forms are easily duplicated. Feel free to choose any of the forms "as is," or change them and adapt them to your specific needs. Attach with each form any assessments and activities that will be shared.

TAG . . . You're It!

Exercising the Herd

Exercise One

Of course, the first exercise is to build the COWs. *(In one-day workshops, I often have participants build what you might call a "mini-COW." Maybe this exercise should be called Calves.)* Get the core team and the elective team together. Have each of the teachers fill in six adhesive notes to randomly represent six topics they each teach during the school year, and put them on a piece of poster board. Teachers look for potential learning connections. Then they should each choose one topic, discuss, and develop a learning connection. Refer to the chart on page 66 for examples of basic learning connections.

Exercise Two

Working in departments, use the COWs and the form on page 233. First, identify a skill set and determine when it is currently taught. Then, look for opportunities to provide additional exposures within the departments' classes.

Exercise Three

Work in teams and use the COWs to identify where the skill sets identified by the departments might be used in the other curriculum areas. The form on page 234 may be useful in identifying the timeline for spiraling the learning connections. Then look for opportunities to create ongoing projects and interdisciplinary units.

Integrated Curriculum Learning Connections Planning Chart

For Correlating Topics, Timelines, Shared Assessments, Focus Activities, Project Development, and Differentiated Instruction.

Connecting Areas, Weeks, Timelines, and Topics
Student Performances: Focus Activities, Reference Points, Shared Assignments, Assessments, and More
Standards Achieved: What Questions Will Be Answered? Attach Assessments.
Differentiated Instruction: Shared Strategies, Multiple Intelligences, Learning Styles, and Modalities

Integrated Curriculum
Learning Connections Planning Chart
For Correlating Topics, Timelines, Shared Assessments, Focus Activities, Project Development and Differentiated Instruction.

CONNECTING AREAS, WEEKS/TIMELINES & TOPICS
wk 11 Rectangular Coordinate Plane | wk 3 Physical Features of Maps

STUDENT PERFORMANCES: FOCUS ACTIVITIES, REFERENCE POINTS, SHARED ASSIGNMENTS/ASSESSMENTS, ETC.
coordinate plane
plot (x, y) points
convert inches to miles using scales
Grid
map of cities
lat + long.
measure distance to cities

STANDARDS ACHIEVED: WHAT QUESTIONS WILL BE ANSWERED? ASSESSMENTS ATTACHED.
PAF 1.3 attach test questi...

DIFFERENTIATED INSTRUCTION: MULTIPLE ... AND MODALITIES USED TO MOTIVATE STUD...
use coordinate plane to f...
Battleship w/ side walk chalk

Integrated Curriculum
Learning Connections Planning Chart
For Correlating Topics, Timelines, Shared Assessments, Focus Activities, Project Development and Differentiated Instruction.

3RD QTR ⇒ Spring Theme – flowers, gardens, insects, birds w/ poetry
4th QTR Summer FREE time theme ⇒ Snack Food Treats w/ Pop art concepts + facts, pouring out

CONNECTING AREAS, WEEKS/TIMELINES & TOPICS
(Visual) Art and L.A.
Time Line: quarterly Topic: Pop Art Paper Maché

STUDENT PERFORMANCES: FOCUS ACTIVITIES, REFERENCE POINTS, SHARED ASSIGNMENTS/ASSESSMENTS, ETC.
ART: Paper Maché Sculpture Activity
create (head stones) sculpture using maché
study Pop Art as an art movement relating to contemporary culture
Apply the words to the sculpture
Note: placement + legibility
Language Arts: Journal Writing entries
Pre-write epitaph; rewrite epitaph; reflection of personal experience w/ creating this personal project
Focus on idea, word choice + sentence fluency.
Shared: ... (ie epitaph) for idea, word choice,

... BE ANSWERED? ASSESSMENTS
... Pop Artists + their artwork and consider its ...'s setting.
... study, free standing paper maché sculptures
... connection betw. visual arts + Lang. Arts

... will be in 6th Grade hall.

...LLIGENCES, LEARNING STYLES
/ Creative writing
Reproduce / Sculpture
/ Role-play
/ Simulations
/ Journal

Integrated Curriculum Learning Connections Planning Chart
For Correlating Topics, Timelines, Shared Assessments, Focus Activities, Project Development and Differentiated Instruction.

- CONNECTING AREAS, WEEKS/TIMELINES & TOPICS
  Spanish + Art - 6th grade. Week 5 - Classroom Projects. Week 7 - 1 point Perspective
  Every Quarter
- STUDENT PERFORMANCES: FOCUS ACTIVITIES, REFERENCE POINTS, SHARED ASSIGNMENTS/ASSESSMENTS, ETC.
  Room Interior - Spanish ideal classroom using a 1 point perspective. For students who have Spanish before Art, use ideal classrooms as a comparison for a 1 Point Perspective drawing. For students who have Art first, Ideal Classroom should be drawn in 1-Pt Perspective for Extra Credit
- STANDARDS ACHIEVED: WHAT QUESTIONS WILL BE ANSWERED? ASSESSMENTS ATTACHED.
  Spanish: Communication B5 and Comparisons H3
  Art: A.8.6, C.8.8, E.8.1, G.8.1, H.8.3, K.8.1
  How can a 1 Point Perspective drawing be utilized?
  How do drawings and language connect?
- DIFFERENTIATED INSTRUCTION: MULTIPLE INTELLEGENCES, LEARNING STYLES AND MODALITIES USED TO MOTIVATE STUDENTS.
  Visual Spatial, Body-Kinesthetic, Interpersonal
  Verbal Linguistic, possibly Naturalist, Logical-Mathematical

Examples of Learning Connections Planning Charts

Learning Connections Planning Chart

For Correlating Shared Assessments, Focus Activities, Multiple Intelligences, and Differentiated Instruction

CONNECTING AREAS/WKS	CONNECTING TOPICS	SHARED ACTIVITIES, WORKSHEETS, REFERENCE POINTS, ASSESSMENTS, ETC.	LEARNING STYLES MULTI. INTEL. and MOD. USED

Learning Connections Planning Chart (SAMPLE)

For Correlating Shared Assessments, Focus Activities, Multiple Intelligences, and Differentiated Instruction

CONNECTING AREAS/WKS	CONNECTING TOPICS	SHARED ACTIVITIES, WORKSHEETS, REFERENCE POINTS, ASSESSMENTS, ETC.	LEARNING STYLES MULTI. INTEL. and MOD. USED
Math: WK 8–9 SS: WK 28–30	Charts and Graphs with Demographics and Elections.	Some of the math charts and graph worksheets will use information from the demographics already studied in social studies, and with election information to be covered later in SS. Shared state test items will be used in both areas in unit tests.	Verbal/Linguistic—predictions Interpersonal—SS Community groups Logical/Mathematical Visual/Spatial—graph, illustrate Body/Kinesthetic—presentations
Math: WK 4 ART: WK 5 of rotation	Line Design with String Art Sculptures	Students will use line designs in math for the base of their string art sculptures. 25% of the math grade will be art sculpture, and 25% of the art grade will be the math designs. Art will use math state test items for angles and measurement in class activities.	Body/Kinesthetic—building sculptures Logical/Mathematical Naturalist—patterns and natural design Intrapersonal—demonstrate, create, etc.
Math—WK 15–16 LA: WK 15	Simplifying Expressions and Writing Sentences	Students will write a cover letter, create spread sheets, and build a portfolio for their bid projects. The Language Arts Math grades will be interdependent. They will share and embed state test items in their activities and tests.	Verbal/Linguistic Logical/Mathematical Visual/Spatial—design a cover, etc. Interpersonal—const. companies Naturalist—outdoor projects, envir.
Math—Music Ongoing	Equations and Formulas with Writing Music.	Students will put equations and formulas to music. The music might be a popular song or an original song created by the student. The students will work on the songs in music, and will have to teach the other students the song in math class.	Musical/Rhythmic—setting to music Verbal/Linguistic—composing Logical/Mathematical Visual/Spatial—illustrating, etc. Body/Kinesthetic—dances Interpersonal—performances

Embedded Thematic Strands
Bid Writing

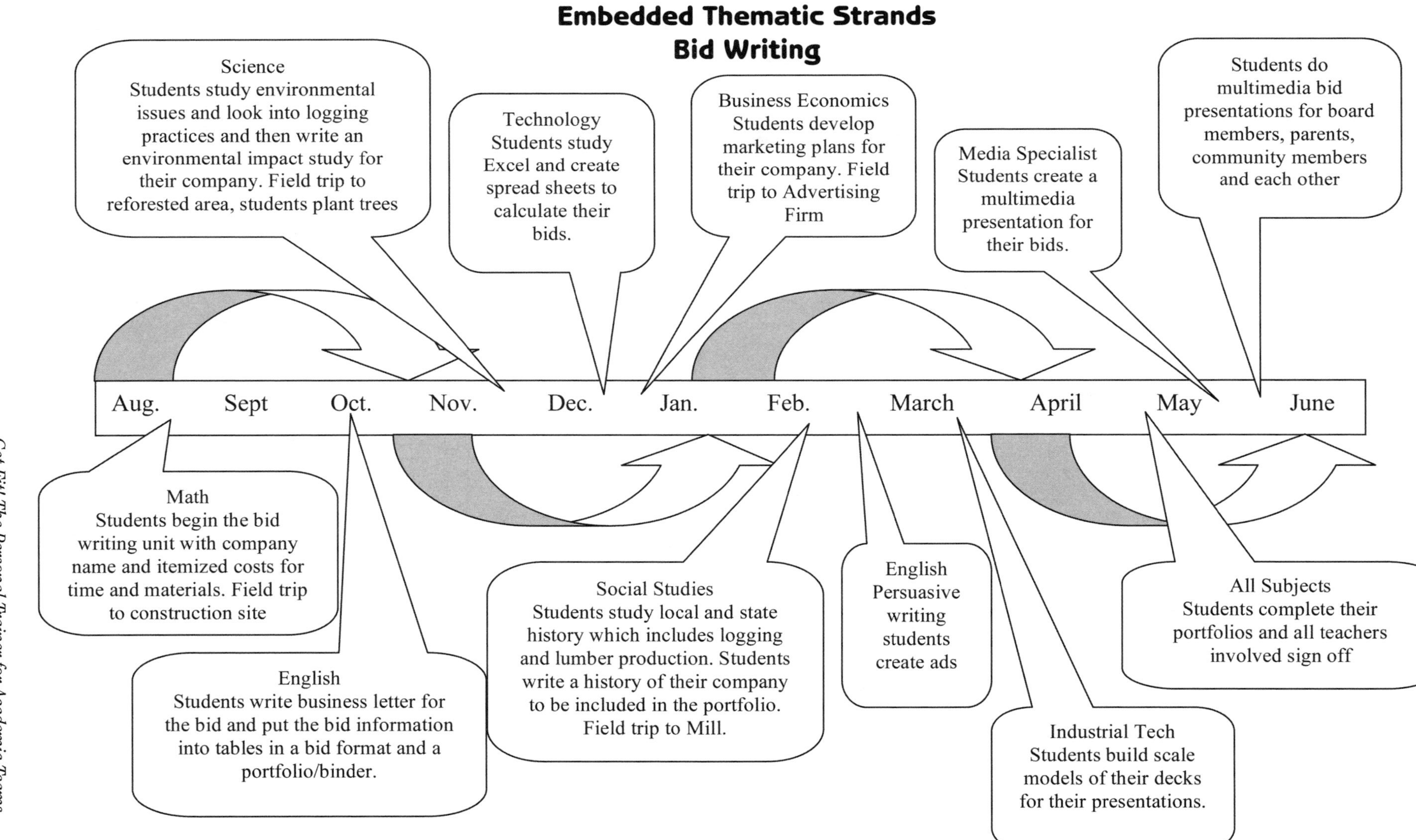

Science
Students study environmental issues and look into logging practices and then write an environmental impact study for their company. Field trip to reforested area, students plant trees
Technology
Students study Excel and create spread sheets to calculate their bids.
Business Economics
Students develop marketing plans for their company. Field trip to Advertising Firm
Media Specialist
Students create a multimedia presentation for their bids.
Students do multimedia bid presentations for board members, parents, community members and each other
Aug.
Sept
Oct.
Nov.
Dec.
Jan.
Feb.
March
April
May
June
Math
Students begin the bid writing unit with company name and itemized costs for time and materials. Field trip to construction site
English
Students write business letter for the bid and put the bid information into tables in a bid format and a portfolio/binder.
Social Studies
Students study local and state history which includes logging and lumber production. Students write a history of their company to be included in the portfolio. Field trip to Mill.
English
Persuasive writing students create ads
Industrial Tech
Students build scale models of their decks for their presentations.
All Subjects
Students complete their portfolios and all teachers involved sign off

Departmental Mapping of Current Skill Placement and Curriculum Realignment if Needed

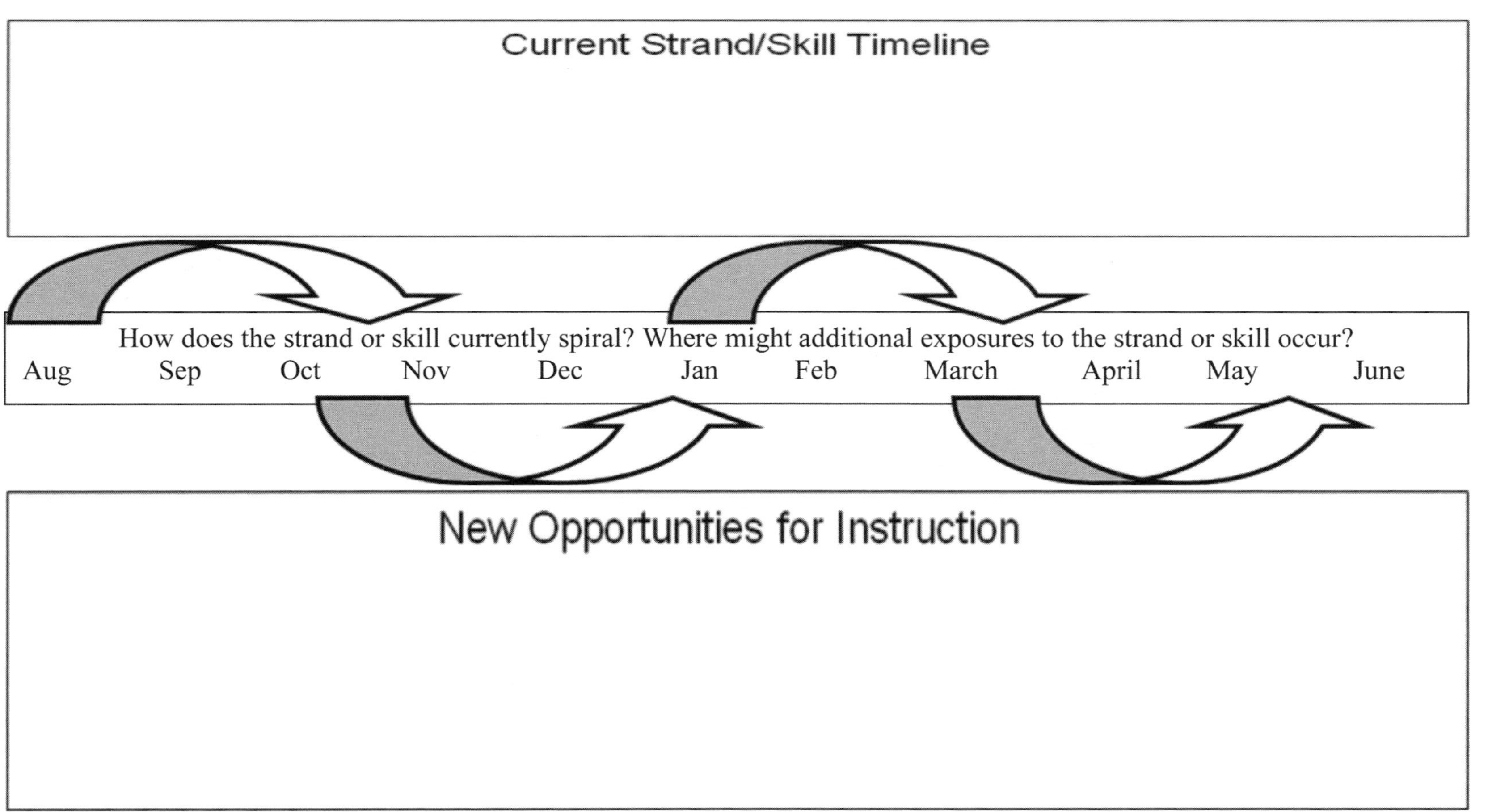

Embedded Thematic Strands
Interdisciplinary and Transitional

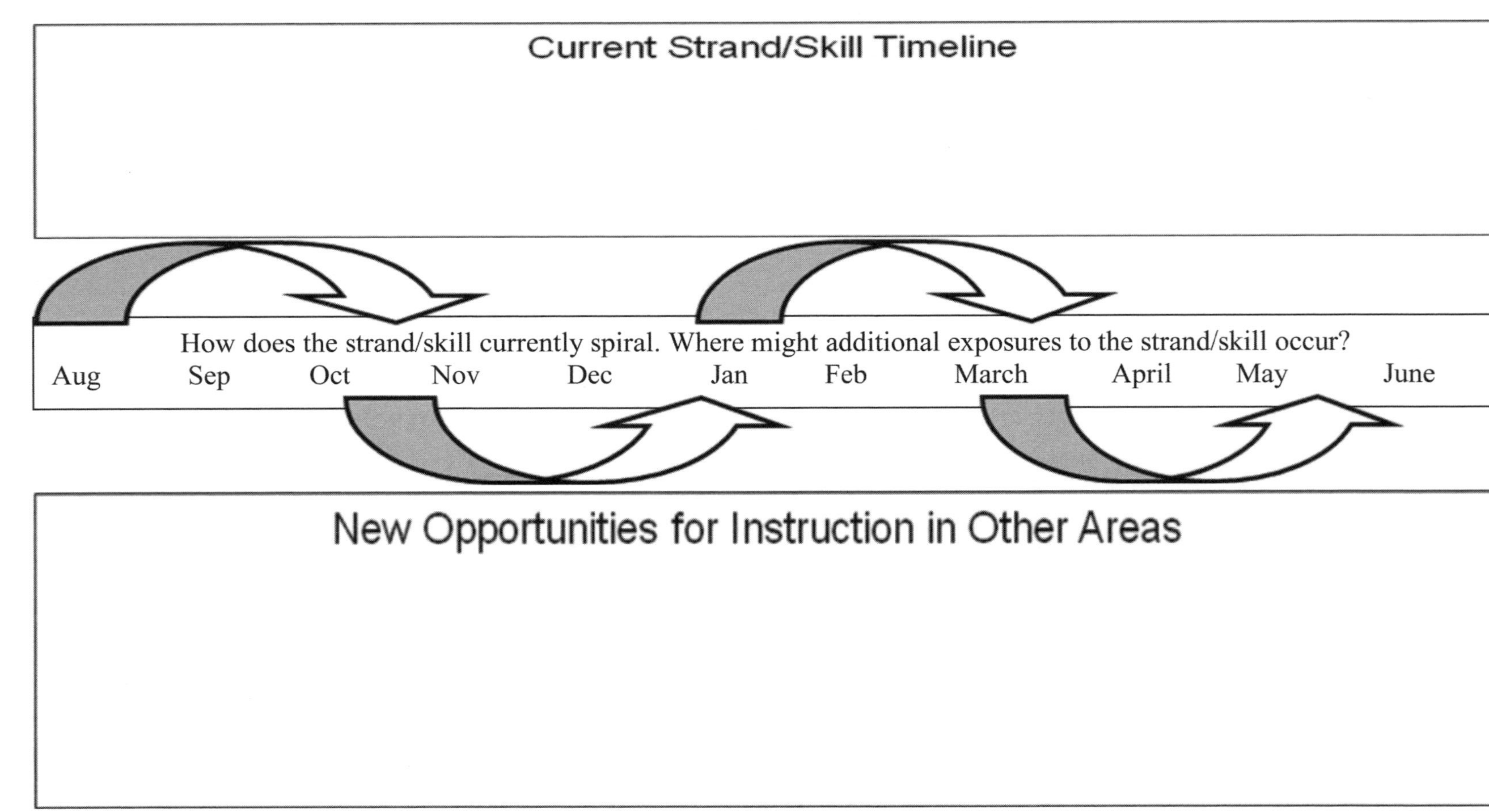

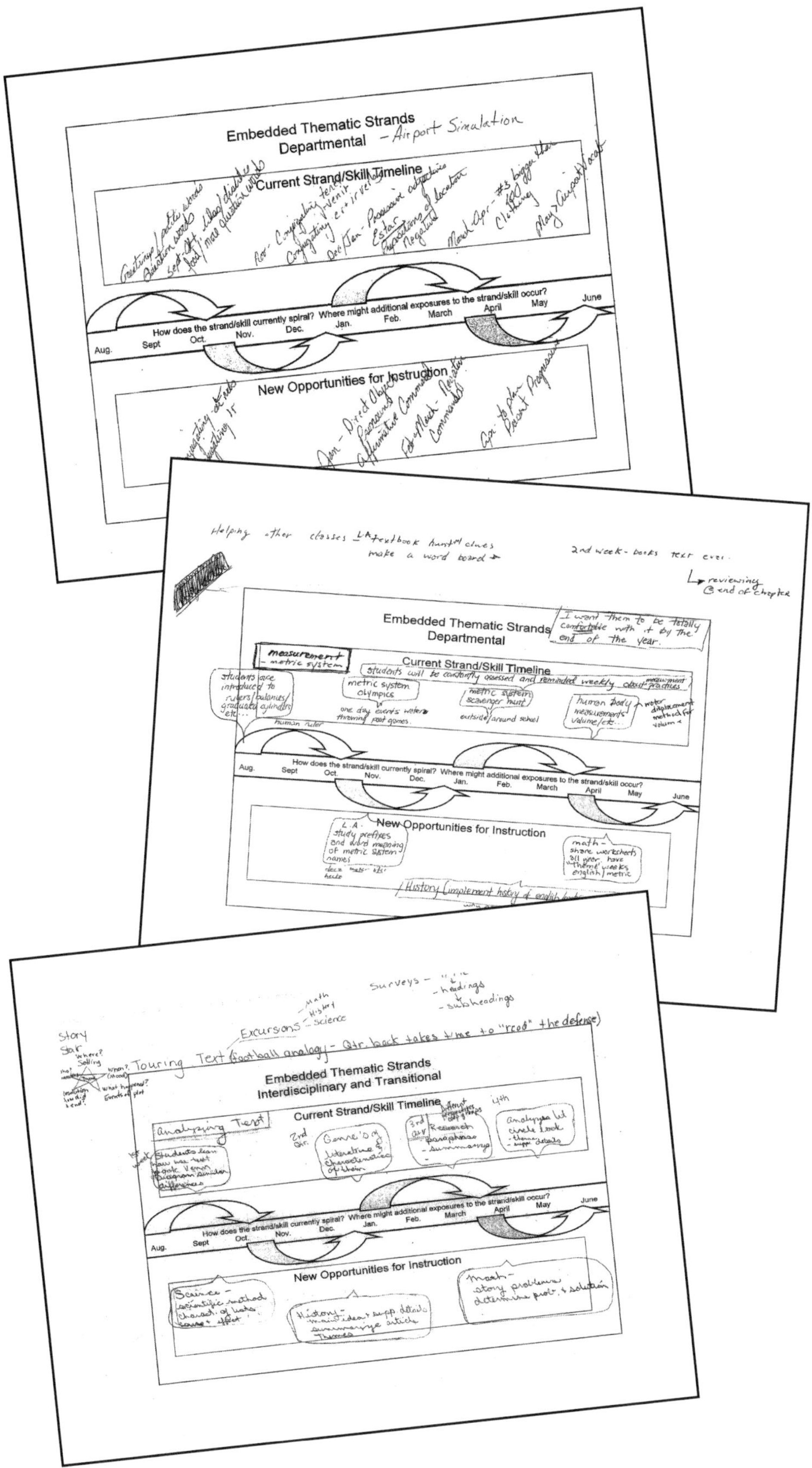

Examples of Spiraling Form

Developing Meaningful Community-Team Partnerships—COMPASS

COMmunity Partnerships Assuring Student Success

Reengaging the Community in Schools

Communities take great pride in their local sports teams. In basketball, when we talk about the "6th man," and in football, the "12th man", we are talking about the fans. Fans are the people that support teams with their presence, their vocal support, their financial support, and most importantly, their common will for the success of the team. If there were no fans, there would be no event. Interdisciplinary teams and schools are no different. They need fans, too.

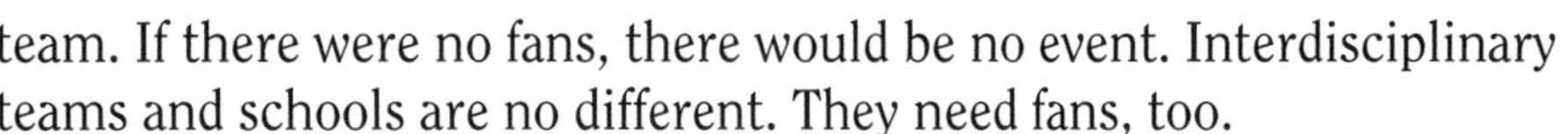

With that in mind, we need to work at developing, maintaining, and expanding the community involvement in our teams and schools. *COMPASS* stands for *Community Partnerships Assuring Student Success*. *(This program is the best way I have found to get the community reengaged with teams and schools in an active and meaningful way.)*

This chapter will outline one way to initiate COMPASS and explain the many positive ways it can and will impact your team and school. COMPASS is an effective way to raise the level of awareness about tremendous demands and curriculum needs that are created by the high-stakes testing. COMPASS will engage the community in curriculum development, especially in relation to meeting the state standards. COMPASS helps teachers and administrators get resources, both human and material, specific to targeted lessons. In these times of increased demands with little or no additional financial support, it is important to find ways to tap the enormous resources available in local communities. *(In other words, we are going to pack the stands!)*

COMPASS works because it is simple, it is based on the business model, and it is symbiotic. The business or community organizations involved in this program feel as though they are getting as much or more from the school as the school is getting from them. This program clearly demonstrates for schools and businesses just how they can support each other, and how they really need each other. Each business that becomes a part of COMPASS becomes intrinsically entwined with the school. *(We are not talking fund-raisers here, but meaningful dialogue and support directly focused on enhancing student performance.)*

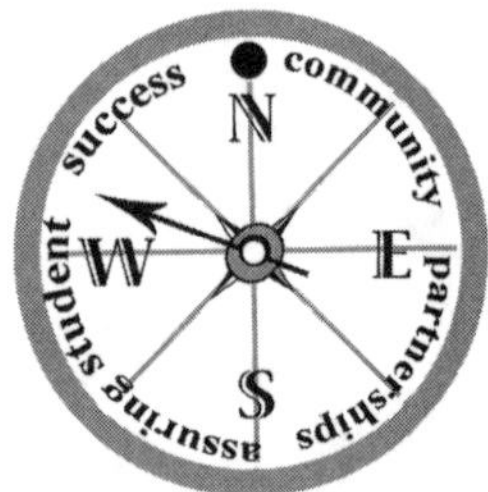

Getting Started

COMPASS is a curriculum-based program, so it is critical that the COWs (curriculum maps) discussed in the previous section be built before beginning the program. *(In fact, I would highly recommend that schools not only have COWs in place, but that they have been in use for at least a year before beginning COMPASS.)* The teachers and administrators need to be very comfortable with the COWs, and need to have developed several "learning connections" before attempting to get the community involved. It takes practice and coaching with developing learning connections to refine the process, and learn to become targeted with the dialogue and efficient with the planning time. Teachers and administrators are going to have to show business people how to use the COWs. *(As with any tool, practice makes perfect, and the COWs are no exception.)*

As you read this book, you will quickly realize that I am all about saving time and energy while getting the job done. One of the many things that teachers and especially businesses like about COMPASS is how the program is time sensitive. From the beginning, the tasks are clearly laid out, the process is somewhat mechanical, and there is not a moment of wasted time. "Time is money," and COMPASS definitely gets the most impact for the time invested.

FOUR POINTS OF COMPASS

1. Build the curriculum maps (COWs).
2. Find learning connections and realign curriculums as needed.
3. Discuss and develop the learning connections between the content areas.
4. Share the COWs with businesses so they can identify learning connections between the curriculums and their businesses.
    a. Businesses look for topics and skills that are part of the curriculum and that are necessary for success in their businesses as well.
    b. Teachers meet with business members to discuss what form the learning connections will take in the classroom.

Getting Businesses Involved

The maps are built, and the teachers and administrators have been using them long enough to be very comfortable with the system. Now it is time to share the maps with the community, and get them involved. The first task for getting businesses involved is contacting them and setting up times to share the COMPASS concept with them. One way to talk to a lot of businesses at the same time is to get on the chamber of commerce agenda for one of their meetings. Let them know you will need only about 15 minutes of the meeting time to discuss what's happening at your school.

Another way to get the ball rolling is to send out invitations to an open house at your school. This can work really well if staff members deliver the invitations and personally invite the businesses to the open house. One school had a staff meeting to identify businesses in which someone on the staff had a personal contact. Staff members, either individually or in small groups, then visited businesses to invite them to an open house. *(Of course, you know that having really good snacks always helps.)* Make sure attendees know the meeting will take only about 30 minutes. It will also help if you can schedule the meetings to take place just before a basketball game, concert, or some other function. Many of the parents involved with the businesses would be present anyway. COMPASS should also be presented at parent meetings, as most parents work somewhere in the community and can share the program with their businesses.

The most effective way to promote COMPASS—to make appointments to visit businesses and make individual presentations—is also the most time-consuming and labor-intensive. *(This contact assures that the business is comfortable because you are taking the program to them.)*

Start with the goal of having one business involved with each of the curriculum maps. As the program grows, and it will, there will be multiple businesses on each map. One business may want to work with multiple maps. *(It has been my experience that once you get a few businesses involved, the program will grow on its own; after the initial solicitation, you will not have to "sell" it.)*

Making the Business Presentation

Whether you have the businesses in your building, you have an appointment at the chamber of commerce meeting, or you are sitting in front of one business executive, the important question is "What do you say?" Follow this step-by-step formula for your presentation. It all starts with the curriculum maps, so have at least one of the maps with you. If you are presenting at a chamber of commerce meeting, or meeting with an individual business at their site, bring just one of the maps. If you are having a community open house, then display all of the maps. If you are an administrator or district level person, invite a teacher who has worked on the map to copresent.

To begin the presentation, explain what the COW is and show what information is contained on it. Remove an adhesive note and show what information is contained on it. Explain that the number in the upper corner indicates the number of the week that the content is being taught; in the center teachers indicate what is being taught; and the numbers and letters on the bottom represent any state standards that are addressed. Explain that each color represents a content area, a recurring theme, an ongoing project, task, or skill. You want the community to recognize the many uses of the curriculum maps and how intricate and complex the curriculums are.

> XX = number of the week
> Content
> Write large and you will not write as much
> State Standards being achieved

Give several examples of learning connections teachers have already developed. Some important points to include are:

- how teachers share assignments, assessments, activities in two different subject areas
- how students get multiple grades in multiple areas for doing one assignment
- how several learning connections have turned into interdisciplinary ongoing projects and, occasionally, interdisciplinary thematic units

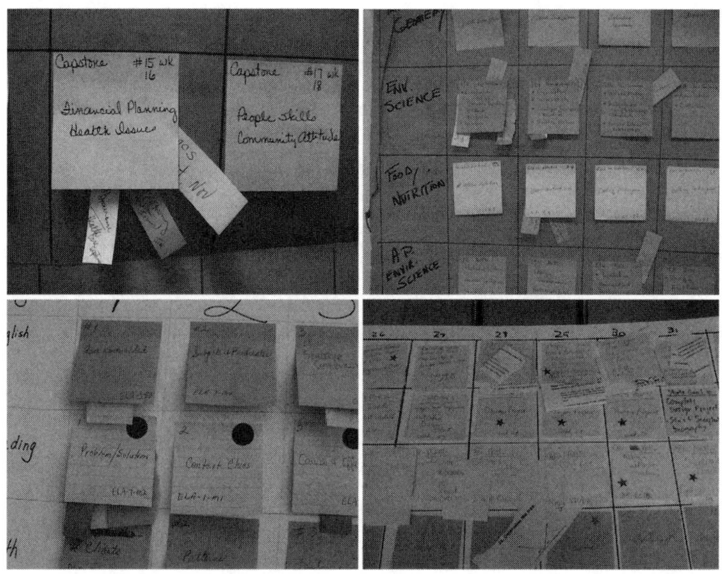

Share sample maps with the businesses to demonstrate learning connections, how the dots are used, and correlation of the sample state assessment items with the curriculums.

Explain how the maps help align curriculums in all areas to ensure the school is addressing all the state standards. Show how test items are actually attached to maps. Share a few of the questions right off the map and encourage businessmen to look at the kinds of questions that are on the state assessments as they look over the maps. *(You want them to know what topics are on the state assessments and what the format of the test is. The community will be impressed with the fact that you have done this type of item analysis.)*

Discuss the dots and tabs and explain what they mean. Demonstrate how the team is tracking the use of technology, the media center, and writing across the curriculum.

Share the development of ongoing projects and how "themes" are developed from learning connections.

Invite the business executives to look over the COWs and read the different topics that are taught in each of the subjects in each of the grade levels. Suggest they look for any topic or skill listed on the maps that they also use in their business. For example, the business may have inventory sheets that would be great examples for students learning to solve problems involving percent of increase or decrease. Students respond to "real" applications of the skills they are learning. So a real sheet from a real business where workers calculate the percent of increase or decrease of sales would be a valuable learning connection. The resulting math homework assignment becomes more relevant to the students.

As the executives look over the maps, give them a set of colored stars or tabs *(You could let them choose the color they want.)* to mark topics for which they might have real-life examples. Business support can take four forms.

a) Executives might share stories or verbal examples of how the skills are used in their business. That way teachers can share real-world stories that people from the business have shared with them to enhance their lessons.

b) Businesses might share materials, such as providing copies of bid sheets, estimate sheets, or form letters to be used in the classroom. They might share instructional videos; for example, a business might have instructional videos for lab safety. Using a safety video from a real company shows students that being safe in their science labs is preparing them for possible jobs in real lab settings. The business may also have pictures and brochures describing the application of different skills.

c) The business person might come in and talk to the students personally about a particular topic or skill. Instead of having the fire department come in and generally talk being firefighters, they could come in and do presentations on PSI or flammable compounds as the students study those topics. The students get a real view of the skills involved in different professions, if the professionals visit when students are actually studying those particular skills.

d) The business might provide onsite experiences for the students. The "field trip" experiences students take to a business through COMPASS are tied to specific skills they observe and study. The students in an English class might visit the newspaper several times in a year. They might make one trip to look at the editing process when they are editing and doing revisions in their class. Later, they might visit to look at the distribution process as a part of their business exploratory class. A third time, they might visit to look at advertising as they study persuasive writing in English. Field trips are targeted toward specific skills, and not all students will go on all field trips. Some students will sign up for the editing trip, others for advertising, and others still for a look at reporting, depending on what they are doing in English classes and what exploratory classes they are taking at the time.

WAYS FOR A BUSINESS TO PARTICIPATE

1. Share stories and examples with the teacher to use in the classroom to make the lesson more real and relevant.
2. Share *hard-copy* examples that show one application of the skill in the business. This might include the forms the business uses, pictures, videos, and brochures.
3. Someone from the business visits the class to share stories and examples in person and to demonstrate how a particular skill is used in the business.
4. Provide field experience opportunities. Students visit the business to view and actually experience firsthand how the skill is applied in the business.

A Closer Look at the Four Types of Involvement

Shared Ideas

The manager of a lab at one company shared stories of accidents involving workers in their laboratory setting. The stories gave the science teacher real-world examples of events that had actually occurred. Instead of using hypothetical situations, the teacher could pass on actual descriptions of events that were shared by a manager with a real name at a real company in the students' community.

It is fine if the manager of the lab is not comfortable coming in and meeting with the students. The manager gives the teacher the next best thing, real-world examples to use in the classroom.

Teachers must develop relevant examples as they are trying to teach a concept. They draw on their own personal experiences and do research to develop additional examples to demonstrate concepts. Often, examples are right there in their own community. A learning connection with a business can help the teacher find the examples in an efficient and effective way.

Shared Materials

As a business looks at one of the COWs, another thing they might do to help develop a learning connection is to share hard copies of documents from their business that might demonstrate or apply a skill from the curriculum map. For example, a business might share examples of forms for bids or inventory that the teacher could use in class. To have the students take inventory of the materials in the science room, the students could use an inventory sheet from a local business.

Shop and lab safety are always important considerations that many students do not always take seriously. Companies have safety videos and follow-up tests that new employees have to view and take. Using these videos demonstrates to students that shop and lab safety are not just ideas the shop teacher or life skills teachers invented. In fact, to get a job at many businesses, students will have to understand and demonstrate knowledge of job safety.

Almost every business has forms, letters, brochures, and videos that help demonstrate and apply many of the concepts taught in schools. In some instances, the students may help with editing or developing brochures for businesses. *(One group of students in Louisiana actually made a television commercial for a business, doing all the writing, editing, acting, and video. Talk about producing for the real world!)*

#3

Classroom Visits

Having someone from an irrigation company or the fire department come in and do a presentation on PSI demonstrates a real-world application and puts a face to the concept. One school had the manager of the produce section of the supermarket talk to the world geography class about how produce is bought from regions all over the world. It amazed the students to realize where the produce they ate was grown, and what logistics were involved in getting it to the grocery store. They were also surprised at how much the manager knew about world politics. The manager explained he had to reference CNN and the Internet every night for information on global markets and global weather.

Live demonstrations in the classroom by someone in the field are an optimum way to demonstrate a skill or the use of a skill. The traditional "Career Day" presents business people from different types of careers talking about their chosen fields. The students may or may not be studying something pertinent to the fields at the time. With a program like COMPASS, the business people in the field come in for particular lessons and to demonstrate particular concepts or skills. They may share examples many times during the year. *(That way "Career Day" can be almost every day!)*

Another very positive aspect of the business person visiting the classroom as part of a learning connection is that the business person has the opportunity to choose the topic they are going to be talking about. This makes them much more comfortable and takes a lot of the pressure off the presentation. Because the businesspersons are choosing their topics, they are much more willing to come in to make a presentation.

Field Experiences

Field trips must be relevant to something the students are studying. When field trips are developed as a part of a learning connection, they are always skill-based. Using the principles of COMPASS, students will visit the fire station not just for a tour, but also to see PSI in action. They will be able to do measurements, see the instruments in use, and actually experience how water pressure is measured. They investigate a specific skill as a part of the field trip.

The business does not give a generic "tour." The students are there to see specific skills demonstrated, so it is easier for the employees of the business to prepare for the visit. Before COMPASS, a managing editor at a newspaper might say something like, "We have students from the middle school coming tomorrow. Be ready to share something about your job and answer whatever questions they might have." The entire newspaper staff would prepare for the visit. With COMPASS, the editor addresses only a portion of the staff and says, "We have students from the middle school coming tomorrow to observe the editing process. Please choose a couple of articles and take them through your process."

Field trips are enjoyable opportunities to get away from school and get out into the real world of work, but through COMPASS students study and observe the applications of the particular skills they are learning. If a business has been sharing examples at the school of how skills are applied in their setting, it is only natural for them to want to let the students see the skills in action at their business. The questions that students ask during the visit are more focused because they are looking for specific information. When students have meaningful questions ready, it is impressive to business personnel.

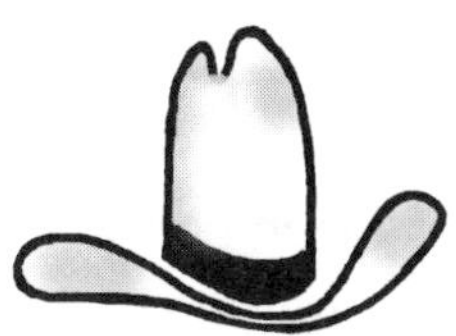

"If you're the one leading the herd, it is a good thing to look around once in a while to make sure they are still following you!"

—from the book ***Don't Squat With Your Spurs On!***

Will COMPASS Benefit the School?

The benefits of COMPASS for schools are obvious and many. The school becomes connected to the community in a real way. As the business partners participate with the teachers to share examples of how skills they teach are applied in the business, the teachers create a more real and relevant curriculum. Students are always asking "When am I ever going to use this?" The businesses give the teachers the answers to that question. The students get to see real-world applications for what they have been learning.

As the business partners work with the schools, it is inevitable that some of the employees are parents of students at the school as well. The more business relationships that schools develop, the more parents will get involved via the business, and even more families begin to become reengaged with the schools. Grandparents, uncles, and aunts who work at a business often get involved, so even extended family members are working with the schools.

The business often provides the classroom with materials to make the lessons more real and relevant by demonstrating how the skills are being used at the business. If a business provides business letterhead when students are writing business letters, it is great advertising for the business, as well as an authentic application of skills for the students and teachers. *(Imagine 150 students all taking home letters with the name of a local business on them.)*

As more people from the businesses come to the school to do presentations, bring materials, and supplement instruction in a variety of ways, the school benefits from having more adults in the building. These are also adults from the businesses that the students know and recognize as helping with the instructional program. Having extra adults in the classrooms, in the hallways, and in the cafeteria is always a good thing for any school. So not only does COMPASS generate supplemental materials for teachers, the program also generates human resources that are invaluable.

Finally, by working with businesses, schools are able to stay on top of current business trends. In that way, schools teach **current** applications of skills in the real-world setting. It is difficult for schools to access the latest business applications of technology due to financial considerations. If businesses come into the school, and occasionally students go into the businesses, the businesses can demonstrate the most current technology applications. Business partners can help schools stay current with the applications of skills teachers are trying to teach. *(And COMPASS also develops in the businesses a great amount of empathy for the schools.)*

COMPASS Benefits Schools

★ Makes curriculum real and relevant
Businesses provide actual examples of the application of skills taught in the curriculum.

★ Connects school with the community
The program creates a symbiotic relationship between the school and the businesses in the program.

★ Re-engages families in the education of students
Many family members work in the businesses that participate in the program.

★ Supplements school resources—human, materials, field trips
The school uses hard-copy examples from the business.
Business people come to the school to help teachers deliver the curriculum.

★ Updates the school on current trends in business
The school and the curriculum are constantly being updated with current business practices.

★ Helps the business community understand the educational system and its challenges
The business community gets a firsthand look at the resources the school has, as well as the challenges and demands the school faces.

Will COMPASS Benefit Businesses?

The success of COMPASS is due in large part to its positive benefits for businesses. It is a very cost-effective public relations program for businesses. Business communities in the past have supported schools, but they have lacked a tool to identify how, when, and exactly where their assistance would be most helpful. They needed an efficient way to determine how to collaborate with the school.

COMPASS targets business and community involvement precisely so that the discussion and development is done effectively and efficiently. After the initial meeting to let executives understand how COWs work, the business takes the COW to the place of business for a week or two. The business selects appropriate topics and specific skills to make a learning connection. Meetings with the team to develop the learning connection do not take a lot of time. Both parties know what the topic is and come prepared. They have a targeted discussion. These meetings are usually no more than 30 minutes and most often do not even take that long. Everyone appreciates meetings that get right to the point. The teachers and the business people will share what they have with each other, discuss what format the business support will take, and the meeting is over in short order.

Businesses can also get information about their business out to current and future consumers through COMPASS. As parents work with their children on skill applications provided by a business, they are more likely to support that business. Down the road, the students are going to be adult consumers, as well. So the students will leave school with up-close and personal information about many of the businesses in the community.

Soon students will be in the workforce. Working with the business community in school helps students become aware of the specific cognitive skills they are going to need to be successful employees. Another equally important return is that they also get to know the affective skills (soft skills, people skills) that are so critical for success on the job. The business people will certainly talk about things like getting along with other employees, being empathetic with customers, getting to work on time, and having a good attitude. Of course, as students begin to develop these skills, they are also more successful in school.

Students become aware of the community service which a business is already doing, and can often work with the business to take the service to a higher level. On the other hand, the business will become aware of the community service projects in which the teachers and students are involved, and will often work with the team on their projects. Their community service becomes service learning. So, in addition to collecting food for a food drive, the students are studying the economy and the causes of homelessness.

Students can often help the business in a real way. In one school, the students created a commercial for one of the local businesses that was shown on the local television channel. In another school, the students, with the cooperation of several businesses, planned and built their own city park. The city donated the land, and the students created a park for endangered species of trees. Imagine the learning connections that came together as they developed and maintained a city park. The park is a year-round commitment, and so then are the learning connections.

Through COMPASS the business community develops an understanding of the demands on today's educators. The more time business people spend in a school, the more they see the really great things that are happening. The business community becomes an advocate for the school, and can help dispel rumors and mistruths that sometimes get going in the community.

COMPASS Benefits Businesses

★ Great public relations

Business expertise and resources help teachers teach and students learn.

★ Cost-effective way to advertise

Imagine 130 students working with supplies provided by a business.

★ Preparation of future employees

Students will be in the work force at some point.

★ More knowledgeable consumers

Students share with parents what they have learned about the businesses and their products.

★ Better understanding and appreciation in schools of the challenges and needs of business

Students and teachers get an up-close and personal look at businesses.

★ Supplement business resources

The students can develop advertising and do number crunching for the businesses.

Students can create posters and put together print and television ads.

Schools can become off-site learning centers for businesses.

★ Better understanding of the education process

Businesses learn about learning.

Businesses become more "brain-based" after working with the educators to develop curriculum and assessments.

★ Community service

Businesses report their employees increase involvement in community service projects after getting involved with COMPASS.

A strong COMPASS program increases the likelihood that school bonds will be passed when they are presented to the community. Imagine the impact of businesses making calls, posting signs, and taking ads in the various media in support of the bond issue! If the business community is actually in the schools and sees what is happening from the curriculum up, it will have a much greater insight into the school's needs.

Showcase the Program and Celebrate the Success

Community breakfasts are one great way to get the business community and the school together with the parents and other interested community members. The school can sponsor the breakfasts and highlight the businesses and the specific lessons that had been developed through the learning connection.

When showcasing teaching units developed with the cooperation of the business, it is, of course, great to have some of the students and teachers that were involved as part of the presentation. I encourage teachers to take lots of digital pictures of students working with the businesses for the local newspaper and PowerPoint presentations. Create handouts—another real learning connection for students—for the breakfasts, including some of the student work and assessments in the unit. It is important that the state-assessed skills be highlighted as a part of the presentation.

Another way to bring heightened understanding about the responsibilities of the teachers and the members of the business community is through teacher-employee switches. Students may participate in shadowing experiences, but it is also valuable if teachers spend some time in the business setting. It is also invaluable for the business to understand what it is like to try to get a student to understand a concept.

One school I know lost a science teacher to a business. The business offered the science teacher a job after the science teacher had spent some time at the business. The school lost a science teacher, but gained an enthusiastic advocate for the school in the business!

Celebration field trips are a way for students to share their success with the people at the business. The business people see and appreciate what the students have learned by applying the skills in the business setting. Of course, a plaque or some sort of framed certificate of appreciation presented to the participating businesses during student visits is always appropriate and appreciated.

There are many more ways to get everyone together. Don't forget to take the opportunity to have fun with staff-partner activities. It is nice for the adults involved in the learning connections to get together in a more casual setting to meet and talk. One school sponsors staff-partner ski evenings at a nearby ski resort once a month during ski season. In another school, the teachers have formed softball teams with the business partners and compete in the local city softball league.

Putting All the Pieces Together

There are a great many pieces to the successful school puzzle.

- Schools want meaningful curriculum choices for all students.
- Schools need more resources for teachers.
- Schools want parents meaningfully involved in the school (more often than just for parent-teacher conferences).
- Schools want the business sector to develop more ownership of school success.
- Schools want every person in the community to become a true stakeholder in education, and to feel vested in and responsible for the school's success.

COMPASS can be the program that pulls all of the divergent puzzle pieces together. Remember, parents work in many of the various businesses in your community. So they are often the ones that are looking at the COWs and discovering the learning connections. That means that some of the business people who will be coming into the school to develop the shared lessons, make presentations, and arrange field trips are also parents. The parents then become more actively engaged with the school. They will see ways they can contribute and feel ownership in the school. They become more responsible for schools' success, as well as their own child's. Since the relationship is built on helping with lessons and shared benefits, many of the parents will continue to work with the school after their child has moved to high school or college. Developing long-term relationships is one of the positive consequences of this program.

COMPASS will help teachers get the right resources at the right time. The COWs provide a positive way for the community to see what the teachers are doing and when they are doing it. So any assistance an individual or business may provide will not only be appropriate, but timely. The curriculum maps are great communication tools, and COMPASS encourages their use!

TAG . . . You're It!

Go Round Up the Herd!

I am going to assume that your teams have COWs in place and in use. Your staff must be comfortable with using the COWs before trying to develop learning connections with a business. If you are not, go back to Chapter 3: Interdisciplinary Curriculum Development. Round up your COWs and develop some learning connections.

Group Exercise

Invite a business to come in and view your COWs. Look for possible learning connections between the business and your curriculums. Have the business use colored dots, stars, or tabs to indicate potential learning connections. Take the COWs to the business if business personnel cannot come to the school. After the business has found several possible learning connections, pick **one** to discuss and develop. Discussing and developing one learning connection at a time with the business partners will keep the teachers and the business from becoming overwhelmed.

Meet with the appropriate person(s) to develop the learning connection. Determine how the lesson will look.

- What will the teacher use from the business to demonstrate the concept?
- Will it include some hard-copy example or reference?
- Will someone from the business do an in-school presentation for the students?
- Will there be a field trip or visit to the business?
- What combination of these possibilities might be used?

The teachers should keep the business up-to-date as the unit progresses. Let the business know how it's going, and if possible, send samples of what the students are doing with comments from the students to the business. Invite your business partners to come watch even if they are not going to be presenting. Finally, send a thank-you letter with a portfolio of sample work from the unit when it is completed.

Establishing Team Identity

Putting the *Community* in Small Learning Communities

Team identity is a critical part of the team success. A common attribute among unsuccessful students is that they tend to be more disenfranchised than successful students. Students who belong to school organizations like sports and clubs also feel more ownership in the school and are invested in the school's success. One of the goals of teams is to get students on each team more invested in school. There are many ways to help make that happen.

In clubs and sports, students participate in a common activity; but coaches also invest time and effort into developing team identity with team T-shirts, jerseys, logos, banners, handshakes, cheers, songs, and even rallies to energize the members. The business community expends a tremendous amount of time and energy in what they often call "team building" or "community building." Visit the business section of any major bookstore and scan the books dedicated to these topics. The business community knows that the more each person in a business identifies with, and is invested in, the business the more successful the business is going to be.

Academic teams can provide this identity within the larger learning community of the school. The trick is to get the students on a team invested in the success of their small learning community. An advisory program is the perfect place to develop this ownership with team-building activities. If you do not have an advisory program, your team will have to take time to work on team identity within your academic schedule.

Developing and maintaining the team identity should be a regularly scheduled team-meeting topic. Teams should use their team name whenever it is possible and applicable. No business would send out any communication without its name and logo on it. Teams should make the team name part of the common paper headings when they are developing their common policies. A social studies project should be a *(Team Name) social studies project*. The team name should be included on any cover page.

Team celebrations for student accomplishment, as described in Chapter Six, are another way to recognize the team. *Thumbs Up* certificates should carry the team name. Team parent nights remind

Team T-Shirts are a great way to develop team identity!

parents that their children are a part of an interconnected group within the school's community for learning.

A team newsletter is one more place for the team to present itself to the parents and community as a cohesive unit. The newsletter should place the team name and logo prominently, and the articles should reference what is happening in the team's classes. For example, the Tiger team will report in the team newsletter what is happening in the Tiger science class and the Tiger math class.

Team Résumé

The teachers on an academic team should present themselves as a team, and a great way to do that is with the team résumé. A team résumé is just what the name implies. The teachers on the team have very impressive individual credentials. A team résumé pools all of those impressive credentials and presents a cumulative picture of the team's qualifications. So the teachers on a team introduce themselves to the parents in the team newsletter. The team describes itself with information about its qualifications. *(A labeled digital photograph is also helpful!)* For example, the team might list the total number of years of experience its teachers have. *(One team calculated the number of students they had taught among them; because they were a fairly "experienced" team, the number was quite impressive!)*

The teachers might include how many colleges they have attended, and how many professional certifications they have between them. They might list the extracurricular activities they sponsor or coach. The teachers could also list the types of jobs they have outside of education. *(In one of the schools I work with, the teams listed fun facts in addition to the professional ones. One team listed the number and types of pets they had, and another listed their favorite hobbies.)*

The team résumé is fun for the teachers to complete, but it also verifies for parents the team's qualifications. The cumulative résumé demonstrates that the team of teachers works together.

Team Banners

Countries, cities, and even armies always have their banners or flags prominently on display. Imagine if each academic team created a banner for its team and displayed the banners in the gym for athletic events, at each football and soccer match, at concerts, plays, and other performances. The banner is another way to demonstrate team pride! You could "retire" the banners at the end of each year. Have a ceremony and then put the retired banners on display around the school. Whether teams create new banners each year or use the same banner from year to year, the banner is one more positive symbol of the team's identity.

THE TOP HATS
AT THE HEAD OF THE CLASS

Team pride can be demonstrated with the team banner.

Team Puzzles

The team puzzle is a creative way to establish team identity. Teachers (or a small group of students) write the team name on a large sheet of butcher paper and fill in the letters with paint or marking pens. Then lines are drawn to form puzzle pieces. The letters in the team name should remain intact. The finished product will look much like a very large puzzle of a team banner that has been put together.

Then the team makes a copy of the puzzle by placing another piece of butcher paper on top and tracing the original. The copy is cut along the lines to create individual puzzle pieces. The letters cut out of the copy are thrown away. When the puzzle pieces are placed on the original, the letters of the team name will show through. Each student decorates one of the puzzle pieces.

Students will see that, just like a puzzle, a team needs every piece to be complete. Each shape is a visual representation of the unique students that work together on the team. Because of the differences, the puzzle is a colorful reminder that a team is a group of individuals that form a cohesive unit.

(By the way, it can also be a powerful experience for a staff to create a staff puzzle as well!)

TAG . . . You're It!

Team Identity

Exercise One

Note: If your team has a team logo and a team banner, proceed to Exercise Two.

Create a team logo and team banner. Students must be involved. You will need to decide on team colors before beginning.
(While you're at it, you might have the students select a team theme song or, better yet, have them write one.)

Exercise Two

This exercise is fun for both students and staff. Build a team puzzle for your team. Write the team name and any other motivational saying on a large piece of butcher paper. Make large block letters and paint the letters with the team colors. Draw curved lines between the letters to create the pieces of the puzzle.

After the original puzzle dries, make a copy of the original. Simply place a piece of blank butcher paper over the original and trace it. Display the original on the wall in the team area. Cut up the traced copy. (You will not use the letters on the copy for the puzzle.) Give students the puzzle pieces. Students decorate the puzzle pieces to represent themselves. Students tape or glue their pieces to the original to complete the puzzle.

Positive Reinforcements

There are many ways to recognize and teach appropriate behavior. Student motivation is critical to student success, and yet, team meetings are all too often focused on consequences for students and not on recognition of their accomplishments. Education is notorious for trying to teach affective skills like respect, responsibility, preparedness, listening, and organization by consequence rather than by direct instruction. Many teachers simply check the appropriate box on the report card indicating that the grade reflects poor organizational skills, not participating in class, not doing homework, and not bringing materials to class. See Chapter 13 on Team-based Advisory Programs for suggestions on how to teach these affective skills.

Positive reinforcements can involve both recognition and rewards. Recognition is a formal acknowledgement of accomplishments. Every time a teacher says "Good job" or "Thanks for putting that problem on the board" the teacher is recognizing student accomplishments. A reward is an additional incentive beyond the original recognition. Every time a student goes to the board for a teacher, the student receives a participation ticket from the teacher. The ticket goes into a jar for that period. At the end of the week, the teacher draws five participation tickets from the jar, and students whose names are drawn receive a prize.

The focus of this chapter is on team recognitions and rewards for students as they develop and use skills that the teachers know will make them more successful. While teachers need a system of consistently administered consequences, using recognition and rewards for appropriate behavior, effort, and quality work motivates students quickly and successfully if the positive reinforcements are consistently administered. The ideas shared here are ones that have been used successfully by teams to motivate students. *(Remember that nearly every business, bank, hotel chain, and airline has a "rewards" program!)*

Here are two important premises to remember as your team develops its common system of recognition and rewards:

Recognitions and rewards work only if students believe it is possible to earn them. So, educators should focus on reinforcing and rewarding both quality work and improvement because every student has a chance to demonstrate one, or both, of these.

Continual improvement leads to quality work. For some recognitions, such as the Thumbs Up certificate, every student has a chance every time to earn a certificate. The available resources limit some other forms of recognition, such as a trip off campus for lunch. When a limited number of rewards are available, every student should still have a chance to earn any particular reward. So the team might implement a "ticket" system whereby students earn a ticket each time they meet criteria established by the team. *(Writing student names on precut pieces of paper in lieu of tickets works well also. In fact, students usually like writing their own names on the slips of paper.)* The teacher draws "winners" from all of the tickets to fill the spots for the off-campus lunch. The more chances every student has to get his or her name in the drawing, the more successful and motivating the recognition/reward system will be.

Share the Work

Every teacher provides positive reinforcements on an individual basis. However, in this chapter the idea is to develop a systemic approach for cumulative team reinforcements and rewards. One of the powerful things about teams is that the teachers can share the workload as long as they communicate with each other regularly and efficiently. *(In my opinion, it is best to divide students into advisory groups. If you don't have advisory groups, divide the students into groups by one of the periods they teach.)*

Displays of Student Work

Putting student work on display in the classroom is always a great way to demonstrate that a teacher appreciates the work done by students. Create a special Top Team Work display area and take the recognition up a notch. If teachers on the team are in close proximity, then the team can designate a portion of the wall space in the hallway for displays of student work. The work on display should show both top quality and good improvement.

Every team should also display student work in areas outside their team areas. The front foyer of the school or the cafeteria is a great place to show off work for schoolwide recognition. Another good place is just outside the gym during basketball and volleyball seasons. When parents know that a particular team is showcasing the work of their members and that it will be on display before and during the games, guess who will want to attend the sporting event?

Anytime there are seasonal events such as choir and band concerts, the entryway is again a great place to put student work on display. Teachers make the display relevant when they tie the student work into the event. Schools with an interdisciplinary approach to developing and delivering curriculum display student work from individual classes relating to the play being presented by the drama club. Student work, relating to the history behind the music, will be displayed for a concert.

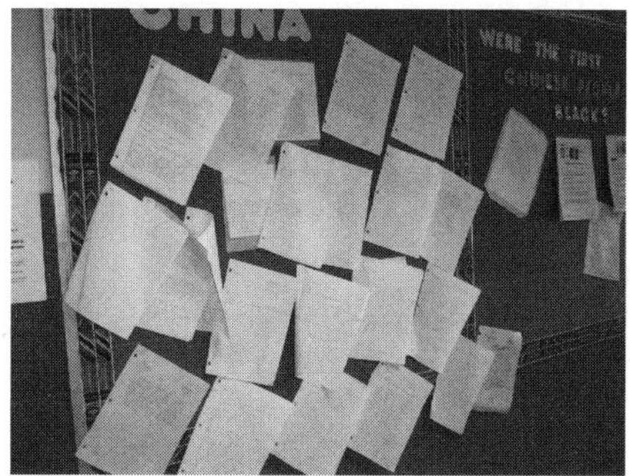

In the chapter on curriculum development, you will learn how to put together ongoing interdisciplinary student projects. Since the projects end at different times in different disciplines, invite parents, school board members, and the community to attend the final student presentation and celebration. Whenever possible, have the students present at school board meetings, or invite the parents in for an evening of student presentations.

Of course, the team should also include student work in their team newsletter. Using a few digital pictures, the teachers can highlight the work the students have been doing during the previous month. The teachers can also highlight upcoming topics in the team newsletter to get students and parents excited about future units of study.

Any article, student work, or photograph that is ready for a team newsletter is also ready for the local newspaper! Schools do not get enough recognition for students' academic accomplishments and the quality of their programs. Sometimes, it is the school's fault. The newspaper is certainly going to cover anything negative that happens regarding the school, but the newspaper is not going to go out of their way to find the positive stories at the school. Rotate the responsibility for providing information to the local paper. Every week, there should be a positive feature in the local newspaper highlighting team and student accomplishments.

Finally, most places of business are eager to display student work. Big retail chains, some banks, and fast food places like to have student-created materials at their location. *(They know it's very good for business. Showing local student work is one of those actions which yields maximum impact from minimal effort.)*

Administrative Recognition

There is no limit to opportunities for the administrative team to provide additional recognition and rewards for the teams. Here are three ways the administrative team can assist the team in providing recognition for worthy students:

An administrator makes an impromptu visit to the team area and finds students in the hallways or classrooms and compliments students on their accomplishments. For this to work, the administrator must give specific recognition to individual students. Simply give the administrative team a list of students and specific reasons for recognition. Remember that the focus should be on quality work and improvement.

Lunch with administrators is another way to recognize student accomplishments. One school sets up a table in front with pitchers of tea and usually a little extra dessert. The administrators and a few teachers eat lunch with invited students. Students get extra drinks and desserts. Another school not only has a table for students to eat lunch with the administrators, but diners also get waited on! The administrators, counselors, office staff, and a few teachers take turns being waiters and waitresses for those invited to eat at the table. The students really love this!

You are invited
Johnny Jones
to lunch with the principal
Wednesday, March 3rd, 12:15 p.m.

3 Banks and retail stores can sponsor part of a rewards program. Give away actual "cash awards" of $5, $10, $15, and $20 in monthly drawings. Add items such as mini-boom boxes and even bikes. In one school, the team draws about 25 names at each grade level assembly each month. *(The students "go nuts" as the names are drawn.)*

Recognizing Students at Team Meetings

Teams often bring students into team meetings to try to help them with behavior and academic issues. It can be very powerful to have students that have done well attend meetings to receive group recognition from all of the teachers on the team. Since the focus is on improvement, as well as quality work, students do not have to be doing well in every class. Imagine a student that is not doing well in one subject, but has improved in others being called into a team meeting to be praised by all of the teachers for improvement in the classes.

Of course, the teachers should do the same thing even if they are not able to bring students into a team meeting. Teachers on a team should share student improvement during team meetings, so that the other teachers can recognize students for work done in another class.

I have found that students who were not successful in my class responded positively when I was able to praise them for work they did for another teacher. Often the spark a teacher needs to light the fire under a student in his or her class can come from accomplishments in another class.

Service Recognition

Some students complete work in affective service areas such as peer mentoring, team tutors, homework partners, student government, SWAT team, adopt-a-grandparent, stream or park clean-up, providing food for a homeless shelter, in addition to the cognitive work in their classes. The more we recognize and reward student efforts in these areas, the greater the participation will be. Of course, the team has to make these experiences available for the students. Many different students are attracted to these activities, and students active in service activities tend to do well with their regular studies. One team uses the form on page 108 to keep track of the number of hours students put into community service.

Students Recognize Each Other

One team I have worked with is called the Bears. They have a program called "Bear Hugs." The *hugs* are half-sheet certificates recognizing students. Both teachers and students can submit names for the awards. Each class has a box and forms for the bear hug nominations. Every other week the teachers remove the recommendations and create official bear hug certificates on the computer. Those being recognized receive the bear hugs during a lunchtime ceremony for the students.

It should be noted that this school has a very good advisory program. During advisory, students receive coaching on appropriate recognitions. Teachers encourage every student to recommend one bear hug at least once a month. Since the team puts an emphasis on the Bear Hug program, it is very successful.

Team Celebrations

When a team has put together a system of recognitions and rewards, it is important to occasionally celebrate the team accomplishments with team assemblies and field days. One team I know takes themed virtual trips twice a year to celebrate their various accomplishments each semester. When I was there, they were taking a virtual trip to Paris. The team had implemented several ways to recognize and reward students throughout the semester, and the grand finale was the trip. By the time of the trip, each student could have earned up to 50 points.

Any student earning at least five points could go on the trip. The first part of the trip was the flight to Paris. The team had the auditorium for the flight so they could show the in-flight movie. During the flight, students earning 40 or more points could sit in "first class." Other students were assigned to business, coach, and economy seating depending on how many points they had earned. The seating in the auditorium was divided into the sections from front to back, and in first class, teachers had beverages and snacks for the students. In business class, the first cup of beverage and a small snack were free, but self-service. In coach class, the students could purchase a cup of beverage and a snack as they entered. In economy class, the students could purchase either a cup of beverage or a snack, but not both.

Students had decorated the multi-purpose room. After the flight, students visited the Eiffel Tower and strolled down the streets of Paris. The students had designed activities for their trip to Paris and had stations set up with the various activities.

By the way, the team tells me that every year the number of students in First Class and Business Class at least doubles by their second trip of the year! The team has never had more than ten students that did not make the first trip and spend the afternoon with one of the administrators. Each year all of the students earn enough points to go on the second trip. That tells me that grades and behavior continue to improve throughout the year at amazing rates.

Team Postcards

Another way to recognize students is to create a postcard with the team logo on it, write something positive on it, and send it to a student's parents. If sending positive team postcards is a weekly topic for team meetings, allow one period (five minutes) for the discussion. The team can send out a lot of postcards each week. If each teacher writes just five a week for the team, they can send at least 20 per week. The reason the team discusses the postcards at the team meeting is that each teacher needs to know what to write about each student that would represent the entire team. If the team simply goes through the class rosters, they can have a positive postcard sent to every student's family in a very few weeks. The team should try to send a couple of positive postcards a year to each student and his or her parents.

Positive Calls or Emails Home

This might be the best of all positive reinforcements possible. Every parent lives for the day that someone from the school calls to share something positive about their child. In this day and time, emails also work for many parents. Either way, communication is a win-win situation. The parents recognize the teachers as advocates for their children when they take the time to make positive calls or send positive emails. The students get additional recognition from their parents, and this magnifies the impact of the recognition. Some teams have their own websites that can also be used for student recognition.

As with team postcards, the team should share the names each week for the positive phone calls or emails so that the teacher making the contact can include information from all of the teachers. The team should attempt to make at least one of these positive phone calls or emails per student per semester. Of course, the more often that these contacts can be made and still be manageable, the better.

Sharing and Documenting Positive Reinforcements

One of the keys to success is sharing and developing ideas and strategies as a team. The team that works together becomes a professional learning community.

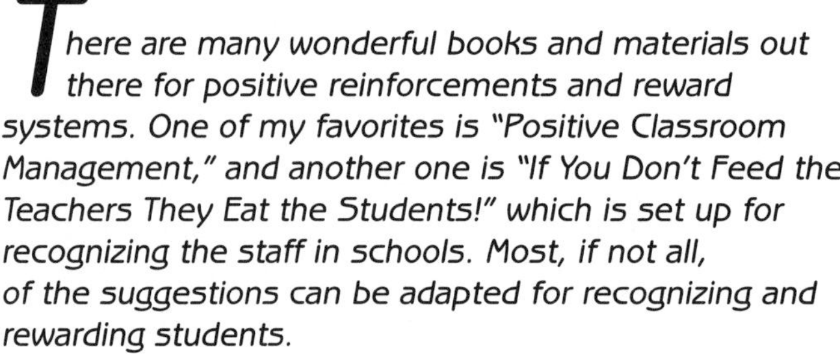

There are many wonderful books and materials out there for positive reinforcements and reward systems. One of my favorites is "Positive Classroom Management," and another one is "If You Don't Feed the Teachers They Eat the Students!" which is set up for recognizing the staff in schools. Most, if not all, of the suggestions can be adapted for recognizing and rewarding students.

In the business section of any bookstore, there are entire rows of books dedicated to recognizing and rewarding employees. It doesn't take too much imagination to adapt most of the suggestions in these books to students.

Just a thought—if the business community dedicates so much time and effort to recognizing and rewarding its workers, there must be a big return in it. The business community does not put time, effort, and big bucks into anything that is not going to get them even more in return. Maybe if schools put more time and effort into recognition and reward systems, they would also see even more positive returns. I really do wonder what schools would be like if they put as much time and effort into recognition and rewards, as they do into developing the codes of conduct and administering the corresponding systems of consequences.

The form on page 107 facilitates team discussion of positive recognitions and rewards, and documents rewards used for specific students. I find that teams often do a very nice job of documenting for parent meetings, and so forth, the consequences they have attempted in trying to manage a student's behavior. It is also very helpful to share positive strategies that teachers have employed.

Positive Reinforcements and Rewards Record

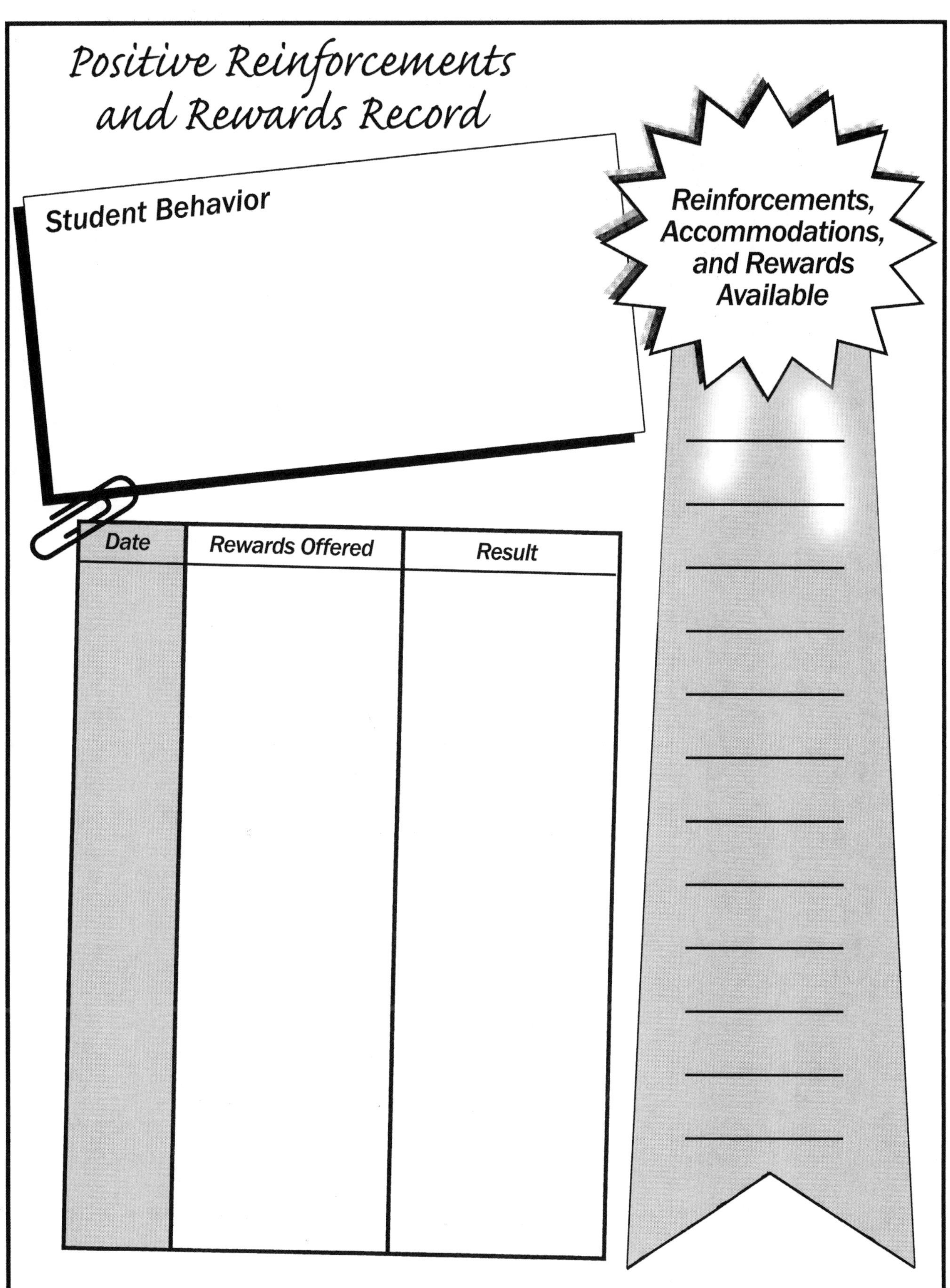

Date	Rewards Offered	Result

COMMUNITY SERVICE LEARNING LOG

DATE	HOURS	LOCATION OF SERVICE	TYPE OF SERVICE	SERVICE SUPERVISOR

TAG . . . You're It!

Developing Positive Reinforcements

Exercise One

In this exercise, team members share what they do individually to positively reinforce and motivate students in their classrooms. The team members can use the Positive Reinforcements and Rewards Record (page 107) to list the positive reinforcements each team member uses. Then, the team discusses these individual systems to see if any of them would be appropriate for team use. Remember, a reward is not motivating for any student who does not have an opportunity to earn that reward.

Exercise Two

As a team, identify the ways that positive contacts are made with parents or guardians of students. How often do these positive contacts take place? Discuss how the team can work together to make more positive parent contacts. Work to increase the number of positive contacts. The ultimate goal should be to make as many, or more, positive parent contacts as negative ones.

Exercise Three

Select an individual student and determine what positive reinforcements have been used to motivate this student. Use the Positive Reinforcement and Rewards Record (page 107) to document the list. What other opportunities could be used with this student? Have all of the teachers consistently tried to apply one system of positive reinforcements?

Exercise Four *(for advanced teams)*

Identify the positive reinforcement systems available and study which students are directly impacted by each of the positive reinforcement systems. Then create an overlapping set of positive reinforcement systems so that all students at all levels of performance are impacted by one or more of the systems.

Thumbs Up for Student Success

A great deal of team time is spent dealing with student-management issues. Teams that spend a significant portion of time on positive reinforcements simply do not have the number of student management issues that teams with a less proactive management policy do. The idea is to help students learn how to stay out of trouble before they get into trouble.

This system of positive reinforcements is also a system for discipline and academic intervention; but because the focus is on the positive, I have included it in this chapter.

Thumbs Up for Student Success

The team as a whole, and each of its teachers individually, are responsible for many students. The task of meeting students' very different needs can be overwhelming. However, teams can provide a level of support that no other management system can provide. Traditionally the discussion at team meetings is about a very small percentage of the students. It is very rare that a team is able to focus on every single student on the team during one team meeting, or even over a period of several team meetings. *(That is what makes the system that I am going to share here so powerful!)*

The system presented here is run by a series of team meetings called ***Thumbs Meetings***. Like all great systems, its beauty is in its simplicity and surprising impact on student performance. During Thumbs Meetings, every student is mentioned by name, and the staff determines what recognition or intervention that student should receive. Most teams run these meetings every two weeks. So, half of the teams in a school run their Thumbs Meetings on the even weeks, and the other half of the teams on the odd weeks. This makes it easier to ensure that an administrator and a counselor are at the meetings.

One of the requirements for successful Thumbs Meetings is the attendance of both an administrator and a counselor. The team meets with the administrator and counselor to evaluate each student member of the team on five criteria. Every student on the team receives appropriate feedback and interventions as needed following the Thumbs Meetings.

Every two weeks each student receives either a certificate recognizing their efforts or a notice recognizing the need to improve behavior or academic efforts, or both. Many schools call these "Thumbs Up" Certificates and "Heads Up" Notices. This system ensures that no students are overlooked for needed interventions.

You will see a lot of "gray area" students receive more support when you institute Thumbs Meetings. The recognition and interventions are based on criteria that the teachers consider as they review the students.

How It All Works

The mechanics of the meeting are quite simple. First, the team needs a roster of students. Schools with an advisory program will want to use the advisory class lists. If your team does not have an advisory program, consider using either the first or last period class lists. The Thumbs Meetings will be held in the last few minutes of advisory or a designated class period every two weeks.

During the team meeting, it is handy to have two copies of the class list. The administrator or counselor reads the names of each student on the team. As each name is read, team members indicate either a *thumbs up* or a *thumbs down*. If the administrator is reading the names, the counselor is the recorder and records the names of teachers indicating a *thumbs down*.

Absolutely no talking is allowed during the first phase of the meeting when the names are being read. The only person talking is the person reading the names. After each name, the caller pauses briefly so the recorder can note any *thumbs down* signals. No discussion is allowed. This is how the team is able to get through a lot of names very quickly.

A *thumbs up* signal indicates that a teacher feels the student is currently showing success in terms of the five targeted criteria. A *thumbs down* signal indicates a concern by a team member in any one or more areas as a student's name is read. Any *thumbs down* requires an intervention.

The criteria considered are: academic effort, behavior, social issues, emotional issues, and personal issues.

Social, emotional, and personal concerns are never part of the consideration for thumbs up certificates or heads up notices. These criteria are included as a part of the discussion because it is critical to provide support for students experiencing difficulties in these areas. So, a student receiving one or more thumbs down signals from teachers due to social, emotional, or personal concerns, would receive the positive recognition for the academic effort and behavior he or she has earned, but the team would discuss what support, such as counseling, might also be appropriate.

Academic Effort

For the academic effort, the question is whether or not the student is giving each teacher his or her best effort in class. This criteria is not based on grades! A positive response is based, instead, on student efforts. Therefore, if a student is trying in a class, teachers would give the student a *thumbs up* regardless of the grade associated with the efforts. Anytime there is an improvement from previous efforts, the student should earn a *thumbs up*.

Behavior

For disciplinary issues, teachers indicate a *thumbs down* if the student is causing any student management issues. In other words, even if the student is in the beginning stages of a disciplinary procedure, the teacher should indicate a *thumbs down*. To be proactive with student management, educators need to know when students are just beginning to cause problems. *(We need to know what and where those problems are if we are to intervene before things get to the referral stage.)*

Social, Emotional, and Personal Concerns

Note: The social, emotional, and personal concerns criteria are particularly important to the counselor.

The teachers consider whether each student is fitting in with his or her peer group as well as might be expected, whether the student is overly emotional, or whether the student has personal issues such as poor hygiene. So, if any teacher has a concern about social, emotional, or personal issues for a student, that teacher would indicate *thumbs down* when that student's name is read.

After all of the names of the students on the team have been read, the recorder reads back the names of the students who received a *thumbs down*. The team with the counselor and administrator, review these students individually. Then the group decides on the best course of action for each student. Everyone leaves the meeting knowing who is personally responsible for each specific intervention.

It is important that the interventions be timely, so the teachers, counselor, and administrator should begin following up with students immediately after the meeting. The day immediately following the team meeting, teachers will give out the Thumbs Up certificates to recognize those students giving their best efforts, and the Heads Up notices for students whose effort falls below the team's expectations. The administrator and the counselor begin follow-up interventions for students needing assistance immediately after the Thumbs Meeting.

The majority of students will receive positive recognition. Most of the schools that use this system have some sort of award to give out to students who are demonstrating academic effort and behaving in their classes. The certificate may or may not actually say anything about Thumbs Up, but should recognize the student's efforts. Sample certificates for recognition and notices for improvement that teams around the country are using are pictured on page 122.

Focus on the Positive

Again it is important to note that this is a team award and the focus is on the positive with an emphasis on improvement. For example, a student may have been receiving mostly *thumbs down* for his effort and behavior. One of the teachers sees some improvement and is able to give the student a *thumbs up*. The bulk of the teachers haven't seen improvement, but as a team looking at the student's whole situation and the entire day, it is evident that there has been some in at least one of the student's classes. The team should always give this student the *thumbs up* recognition. All other teachers will make a concerted effort to mention the specific improvement the student has made in the *thumbs up* teacher's class. As the student goes through the day after the Thumbs Up meeting, every teacher makes a point of talking to the student about the improved efforts demonstrated. Before this system was in place, there was no organized way for teachers to share the gradual improvement of students, and to make sure that every student is being considered on a regular basis.

Always look for some way to motivate students. Sometimes the trick is to know what a student is doing for the other teachers. The Thumbs Up meetings provide a system for sharing information about all of the students, not just the ones causing the most trouble. The system requires that each teacher look for ways in which students improve, so the entire team can build on that improvement.

Many average and below average students have never received any formal recognition for their efforts. When they see that they can earn recognition for their efforts, and that the recognition is based on continually trying to improve, these students start to set higher goals. In fact, that is true of all students.

Setting Goals

Setting goals is an important component of the Thumbs Up system. Every two weeks, students fill out a goal sheet. In most schools, the goal sheet is simply a half sheet of paper that says, "My goal for the next two weeks is . . . ." Students complete the sentence with their goal.

Schools have found that they can keep students focused on a two-week goal more successfully than on a goal that is projected further in the future. The goal should reference what the student needs to do to receive a *thumbs up* certificate at the next Thumbs Meeting. The goal should also be achievable. Teachers should help the students set incremental goals for improvement. Bringing up a low grade, even a little bit *(maybe especially a little bit)*, can be a great goal. Maintaining a good grade can also a very good goal. Goals can also include getting involved with a service learning project or helping other students by becoming a peer mentor.

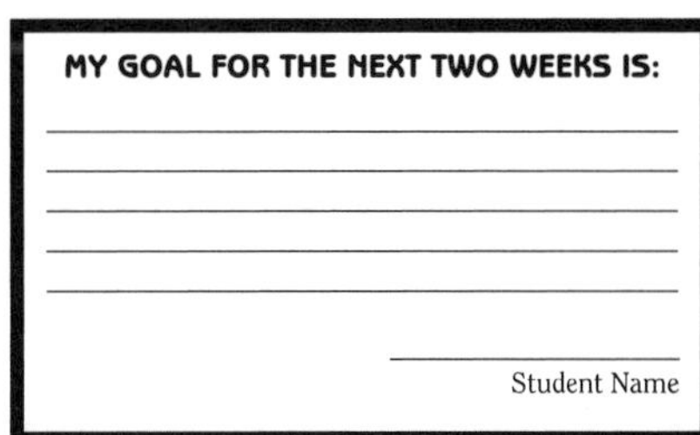
MY GOAL FOR THE NEXT TWO WEEKS IS:

Student Name

Of course, improving behavior may be an appropriate goal for some students. Help students understand how setting and meeting small goals along the way helps achieve big goals.

Exploratory Teachers

It is critical that the exploratory team teachers participate in the Thumbs Up process. The exploratory teachers often see a side of students that the core teachers do not, and the team needs their input to get the complete picture of the student. Teams should have their communicator contact the exploratory teachers to let them know when the team is going to run their Thumbs Up meeting. The exploratory teachers can vote by proxy by sending the team a list of the students they indicate are "thumbs down." Exploratory teachers can go through their class list one student at a time just as the core team does.

Exploratory teachers should send the list of students for which they have concerns to the core team prior to the Thumbs Up meeting. In most schools, this has become much easier because the lists can be sent electronically. Exploratory teachers can simply list the problem criteria by the student's names. Then the administrator or counselor can follow up with the exploratory teachers to get the specifics about the concerns. So the art teacher might put the words *discipline* and *social* by a student's name. An administrator or counselor stops by the art teacher's room to get the specific disciplinary and social concerns and to follow up accordingly.

If the core team is looking for something positive about a particular student, and the exploratory teachers have not indicated a thumbs down for the student, one of the team members may contact the appropriate exploratory teachers to get positive indicators that the core teachers can use. There are many occasions where the students earn a Thumbs Up award because of work done in exploratory classes. With a positive start, the team can use the goal-setting process to get the students to begin to improve in their other classes.

The Interventions

Interventions depend, of course, on the situations each student is facing. The team along with the administrator and counselor review the reasons for a "thumbs down." They choose together the best course of action for each student based on that student's needs.

Academic Effort

If a student's academic effort is one of the issues, there are several options for the team to consider. First, the student's advisor will share the academic concerns with the student during the time when the teacher passes out the Thumbs Up certificates and the Heads Up notices. The advisor will indicate specifically how any improvement needed would look (assignments turned in on time, class participation during discussions). The teacher will also help the student set appropriate, specific goals to demonstrate improvement based on their discussion.

The team may also recommend tutoring in the afterschool program. The advisor will contact the parents to see if the student can stay for the program a few days a week. The team may recommend a "Homework Pal" who checks with the student daily to make sure the student is prepared when he leaves school and to double check with the student in the mornings to get work completed as needed.

The counselor might get involved with the student and work on organizational skills. Other interventions might include additional help time during a lunch help period, and getting the parents to sign the agenda book each day, indicating they have seen the student's assignments. The idea is to get the interventions started at the first sign that the student is not performing academically as he or she should. Do not let the problem drag on until it is very difficult, if not impossible, to help the student.

Behavior—Proactive Student Management

If a student receives a thumbs down for behavior, the team quickly lists the behaviors causing the problem. Generally, this is where the administrator at the meeting goes into action. The administrator makes notes about the behaviors and determines the best time for tracking down the student. The best places for a proactive behavior discussion are the hallways as students change classes, in the cafeteria, in the morning as the students mingle before school, or at the end of one of the periods. *(I always liked to talk to the students in the most public places possible. This is not a referral, so the discussion can and should be brief.)*

The administrator discusses disciplinary concerns with the student and makes suggestions for improving behavior. The idea is to talk with students before they get to the referral stage of the discipline process. The administrator points out specific student behaviors that are a problem, and references specific classes. Very quickly, students will recognize that their behavior is being monitored and evaluated regularly.

I say to students, "I'll be back!" This is why I like to meet in very public places to talk to the students about their behavior. I also want the students to see me return and shake the hands of the students that have improved their behavior. My experience has been that my follow-up meetings after my initial contacts are almost always positive. Another bonus is the effect this system had on my "rounds." As an administrator, I always visited every classroom every day, and I asked other administrators to do the same. We would just step into each class and get a feeling for what was going on. After I had made my initial contacts following Thumbs Meetings, when I would look into classrooms, every one of those students I had talked to thought I was coming into class just to check on them.

It is critical that the counselor be involved with any student experiencing behavior difficulties. A student may make bad choices and not realize alternatives are available. Perhaps home issues are a problem. There are almost always social, emotional, or personal issues involved with misbehavior, and in those situations the counselor is the best person to work with the student. The earlier the counselor is involved with the student, the more positive the effect can be.

The first year that schools put a real focus on the positive reinforcements and early interventions they tend to significantly reduce the referral rate.

In my personal experience, it is not unusual for the written referral rate to drop by half. Of course, this means that grades will also go up significantly. The time teachers had spent on discipline can now be put into instruction!

Social, Emotional, and Personal Issues

Counselors should be involved with any students experiencing behavior difficulties, and the sooner counselors become involved, the more positive the effect can be. Teachers should indicate a thumbs down if they have any feeling that something is not quite right with a student. Of course, if the teachers think the problem is serious at all, they should not wait for a Thumbs Up meeting; they should contact a counselor or administrator immediately.

Often teachers cannot articulate the specific issue. They may say things like, "I am not sure, but Susie has not been participating like she usually does. Has anyone else noticed this?" This statement actually came during one of the Thumbs Meetings I attended as an administrator. Susie was usually the first student to raise her hand and she always volunteered to do work; she was one of those really great students. The teacher had noticed that Susie was still doing well, but was not as enthusiastic as usual. This could mean many things during this time of a student's life. The teacher had asked Susie if anything was wrong, and Susie had said, "No." So the situation was not one of immediate concern that would cause a teacher to go straight to the counselor's office to check on Susie. However, since we read every name aloud, this teacher indicated a Thumbs Down for Susie to see if anyone else had similar concerns.

The response was another phrase you hear often in these meetings, "Now that you mention it, ..." In Susie's case, it was the science teacher that said, "Now that you mention it, Susie didn't volunteer to lead a lab group this time, and she usually wants to lead her lab group. I didn't think anything about it at the time, but she has not been enthusiastic this week." The counselor said she would look into it. After that meeting the counselor stepped into a couple of Susie's classes and noticed that Susie seemed distracted.

The next day the counselor talked with Susie as only this counselor could. After talking for a short while with the counselor, Susie broke down crying; she told the counselor that her dad had left, and her mom had said he was not coming back. Susie's mom told her that they were separated and they were not going to get back together. No one else knew about this, and Susie did not know how to handle the situation. She was embarrassed, confused, and mad. You can imagine how all of the emotions were overwhelming her. Susie felt that she had the weight of the world on her shoulders. The counselor worked with Susie and her mom and was able to provide support.

Wrightstown Middle School in Wrightstown, Wisconsin implemented Thumbs Meetings after a summer in-service where I shared this system with them. During a follow-up visit to the school the counselor, Jen Drobnik, reported how powerful the Thumbs Up system was for her. I asked her if she would take time out of her very busy schedule to email me about how the Thumbs Meetings had impacted Wrightstown Middle. Below is a list of benefits that Jen put together.

The Benefits of Thumbs Meetings

 An excellent tool for communication, the meetings assist teachers in thinking about their students not only on an academic and behavioral level, but also a social and emotional level.

 Thumbs Meetings allow the school counselor and principal to intervene more quickly and take a more proactive role in heading off student issues that might have "snowballed" if addressed later.

 Our change in negative student behavior has a higher turnaround rate.

 Thumbs Meetings present the teachers, principals, and counselors as caring and involved people in the students' lives, creating a positive school atmosphere for the student.

 Teachers see counselors as a resource as a result of Thumbs Meetings, and this serves as a reminder to the teaching staff to utilize their counselor's services.

 Thumbs Meetings assist school counselors in tracking student contacts.

Thumbs Meetings keep me personally very busy. School counselors end their day feeling like they have had a great workout.

In Conclusion

Thumbs Up is a positive, proactive student management system. When a student's name is read, teachers get an immediate mental picture of that student. In the traditional team meeting, discussion about a few problem students can take up the bulk of team meeting time. With Thumbs Meetings, it is impossible for every student on the team not to be a part of the discussion.

Thumbs Meetings are part of the most comprehensive positive reinforcement system that I am aware of. If the Thumbs Up system is run properly, every student on the team has a legitimate opportunity to earn recognition. The Thumbs Meetings and recognitions are scheduled often enough for the students to stay focused. The feedback is every other week, so students focus on the current week and the next week, and then they get cumulative feedback from the team.

When teachers have a positive focus and regularly share accomplishments of students in each other's classes, students receive verbal positive feedback, as well as recognition certificates. Teachers begin to congratulate students for work and improvement in classes other than their own, and that is not always the case in the middle and high school settings. The Thumbs Meeting is an efficient way for teachers to share information about all students and a very effective way to provide positive recognition for all students.

Thumbs Meetings get teachers, administrators, and counselors working together in a cohesive and comprehensive way. Every person attending a Thumbs Meeting leaves with a list of the students he or she is personally responsible for contacting. All students receive either a Thumbs Up certificate or a Heads Up notice every two weeks. It is the personal responsibility of the teacher handing the certificates *(hopefully the student's advisor)* to give each student feedback about their performance. The administrator is personally responsible for meeting with students identified as having behavior issues. The counselor is there to help with any disciplinary issues, as well as social, emotional, or personal concerns.

Remember, administrators, counselors, and teachers continually give positive recognition to students as a part of the Thumbs Up system. When they do have to provide interventions, the follow-up to those interventions is almost always positive. So students are going to see an administrator shake hands in congratulations more often then they see the administrator deal with discipline issues. *(By the way, this only gets better and better as the school year progresses.)*

Please note: Thumbs Up certificates look just like the Heads Up notices. Other students cannot tell what a student has received unless the student chooses to share this information.

THUMBS UP!
FOR A JOB
WELL DONE
TO
#1

TAG . . . You're It!

Thumbs Up for Your Team

Exercise One

(I'll bet you already know what this exercise is going to be.) Schedule a time with an administrator and the counselor for your team and run through a Thumbs Up meeting. You will find that it will take some time at first, but if you practice and stick to the rules, particularly not talking during the first phase of the meeting, the meetings will run smoothly and quickly.

Exercise Two

Now that you have run a Thumbs Up meeting, it is time to practice following up with the students. Each person is responsible for the appropriate interventions described in the chapter. Design the Thumbs Up certificates and Heads Up notices that will be given out to the students. The words Thumbs Up and Heads Up do not have to be on the certificates. Keep the certificates simple. Be sure the team name is prominent.

Proactive Student Management

Introduction

Student management issues usually dominate team meetings. The focus of this chapter is to help teams work smarter and be more efficient when dealing with disciplinary issues. One of first things I coach teams to do is to become proactive with student management. Teams spend a great deal of time reacting to student behaviors, and time can be cut dramatically by heading off student behaviors before the behaviors become serious.

Thumbs Up for Proactive Student Management

The most effective proactive system for dealing with student management is the Thumbs Up system. (See Chapter Seven for a complete description of this strategy.) Using the Thumbs Up process, the team meets with an administrator and counselor every two weeks to discuss each student on the team individually. Every student on the team receives regular feedback as a result of these meetings.

In most systems, the administrators are not very involved with student disciplinary issues until the referral stage of the discipline process. With the Thumbs Up process, the administrators will be involved with students as they are beginning to exhibit disciplinary problems. This proactive approach allows administrators to deal with disciplinary issues prereferral and, in most cases, avoid the referrals for many students. When written referrals are reduced, every minute of that time goes back into instruction. The key is that the team has a manageable system for going through the entire list of students.

Referral Reviews

The team should schedule a specific time during their team meeting to study the causes and effects of referrals received by students on the team. Reviewing disciplinary referrals is the best way for teachers and administrators to share information and evaluate specific strategies for dealing with discipline. Each review is a chance to "norm" the referral process. The team needs to be consistent in the types of behaviors that result in a referral and in the wording used to describe behaviors.

The administrators need to be consistent in the way they deal with types of referrals the team sends them. Sometimes, administrators I have worked with complain about the inconsistency of the referrals they receive, and, on occasion, the teachers complain about the inconsistencies in the ways administrators deal with the referrals. The process I am going to share eliminates all of these issues and provides a quick way to get everyone on the same page.

Schedule time, as a team, for addressing referral studies on a regular basis. At this time, the administrator for the team brings any referrals written by the teachers regarding any of the students on the team. This referral study may be done weekly, and should be done at least every other week so the number of referrals to be discussed does not become overwhelming. The team designates the time and allots two periods (ten minutes) for the process. (See page 25 in Interdisciplinary Team Management for an explanation of periods.) For example, the team might designate the first ten minutes of each Friday team meeting for reviewing the team's referrals. The administrator attends the team meetings on Fridays and reviews the referrals with the team.

The administrator reads the first referral to the team and shares his or her response. The team and the administrator briefly discuss and consider changes for future situations like the one described. Questions might include: "How might the referral have been avoided? Did the administrator deal with the referral in a way that was satisfactory to the teachers? Did the student's behavior change as a result of the referral?

DATE:

TEAM MEETING AGENDA

MEMBERS PRESENT:

PERIODS ALLOTTED	TOPIC	DISCUSSION ACTION TAKEN WHAT IS TO BE DONE?	PRS AND TIMELINE WHO WILL DO IT? WHEN WILL IT BE DONE?

Would the team suggest any changes in the wording for the referral?" The team should not spend a great deal of time on each case; it should try to come to consensus quickly and move on to the next referral. Several things happen as a result of these discipline referral reviews:

The team works as a professional learning community. In this instance, the teachers share specific student management strategies and offer suggestions to each other. There is a longitudinal study built into the process. Since teachers hear and discuss referrals regularly throughout the year, they are able to study which strategies work and which ones do not. Over time, the team will see what adjustments the teachers and the administrators have made as a result of each referral review. If teachers or administrators do not make the suggested adjustments, it will be evident.

The disciplinary referral studies clear up misunderstandings and help administration and instructional staff. The administrator knows that he or she will face the team after dealing with each referral. The teacher knows that whatever is written on a referral will be read aloud to his or her colleagues. If the referral process is to continually improve, the administrator and the teacher need the team's feedback regarding how the referral was addressed.

I was in attendance at one of the referral reviews early in the school year for a team, and one of the referrals that was read happened to be for not bringing a pencil or paper to class. Yes, I know that you probably find that hard to believe, but that is part of what this process is all about. The rest of the team was surprised that this was a referral and, when asked how they deal with this situation, replied almost in unison that they simply give students paper and pencil when needed and move on with class. The consensus at the meeting between the teachers and the administrator was that not being prepared for class would no longer be considered a referral disciplinary issue and would be dealt with by the teachers.

Helpful Forms for Discipline Strategy Studies

The form on page 130 can be used for sharing and documenting the strategies that have been used by teachers to help specific students with their behavior.

The form on page 131 is for sharing disciplinary strategies that can be used by the team or school. It records cumulative actions taken by the team and school to help a specific student with his or her behavior.

Documenting the strategies used by the teachers for specific students can be helpful. First, it provides a list for parents and administrators of the strategies teachers have tried. Secondly, it verifies that the teachers involved have shared and attempted strategies together. Third, if one teacher finds something that works, it is immediately shared with the other teachers and implemented by all of the team members consistently.
(With the entire team on target, student success is ensured!)

The team must address disciplinary issues as they arise. It is important that the team preschedule discipline strategy study sessions so that these meetings are on the calendar and will happen regardless of what else is going on. In this way, the team is able to be proactive and efficient in dealing with discipline issues.

TAG . . . You're It!

Be Proactive!

Exercise One

The team should invite the administrator that deals with their discipline to a team meeting for the purpose of a referral review. Using the process described for reviewing referrals, work with the administrator to review the referrals for the last week or two.

Exercise Two

Schedule a few periods of team meeting time to discuss individual classroom interventions. Teachers can use the form on page 130. Each teacher fills out the form as completely as possible prior to the team meeting. At the meeting, teachers share their individual strategies. The team then picks a student who has been having behavior issues and discusses what interventions have already been tried, and which ones the team will use in the future.

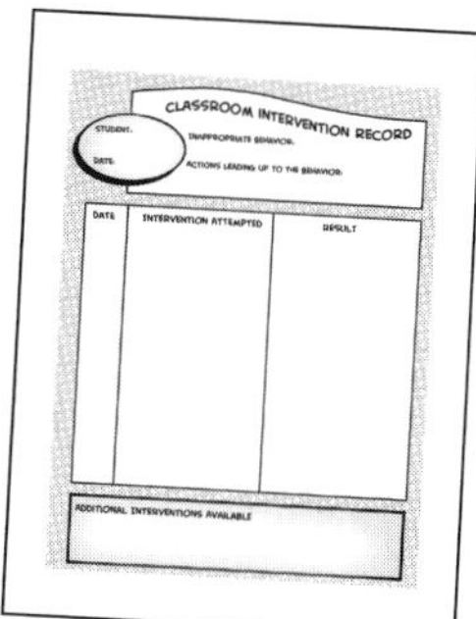

Classroom Intervention Record

Student:

Date:

Inappropriate behavior:

Actions leading up to the behavior:

Date	Intervention attempted	Result

Additional interventions available

Exercise Three

Using the form on page 131, the team discusses team and school interventions. The team should invite one of the administrators to be a part of this discussion. This discussion should include interventions and any schoolwide programs that are available, such as student assistance programs. Discuss how an individual student fits into these options.

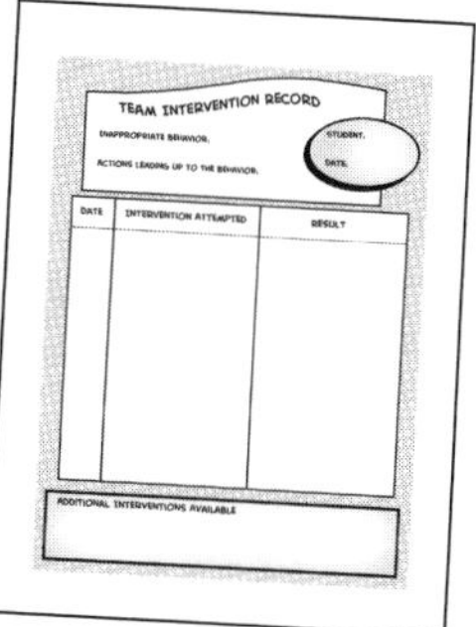

Team Intervention Record

Inappropriate behavior:

Actions leading up to the behavior:

Student:

Date:

Date	Intervention attempted	Result

Additional interventions available

Exercise Four

Develop a team student action plan and a team behavior modification plan. Use the sample on page 132 as an example.

Name:

D

I

S

S

E

C

T

DATE	INTERVENTION ATTEMPTED	RESULT

ADDITIONAL INTERVENTIONS AVAILABLE

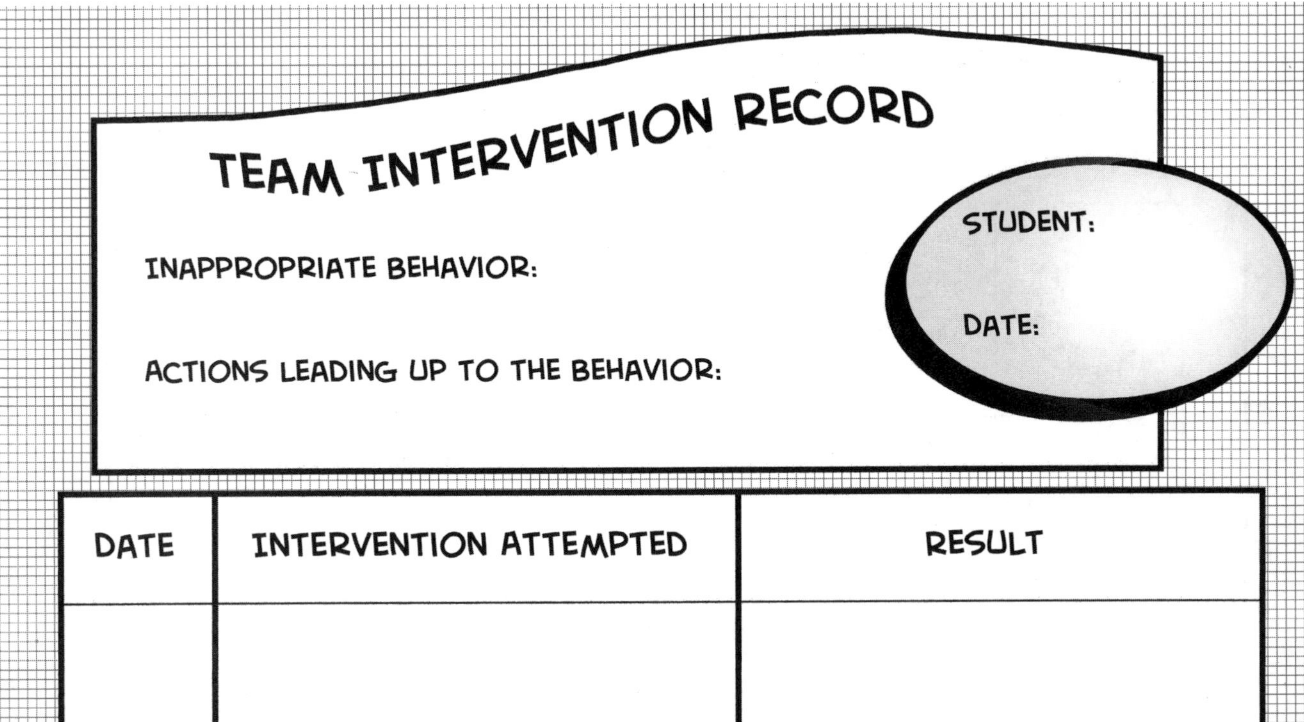

DATE	INTERVENTION ATTEMPTED	RESULT

ADDITIONAL INTERVENTIONS AVAILABLE

Name ____________________

D	Describe the circumstances. Tell when and where.
I	Make an "I" statement. Tell how you felt.
S	Say what happened. Tell what you did.
S	See another side. Tell how someone else felt.
E	Explore the alternatives. Think of several different things you might have done.
C	Choose what you will do next time you find yourself in similar circumstances.
T	Tell your plan.

F.R.O.G.S.

Student Behavior Modification Plan

PHASE I: Student-Teacher conference

PHASE II: Parent Phone Call

PHASE III: (1) Student-Team Conference; "Team Talk"

(2) S.A.D. Form to Assistant Principal

(3) Parent Notification Letter

(4) Possible Student Contract

PHASE IV: Student-parent-team-administrator conference form sent home and signed

PHASE V: Disciplinary Action Mandatory

The phases built into this plan insure the student-teacher-team-parent-administrator participants reflect on the next appropriate step for the benefit of the student. However, if the severity of a student's behavior warrants immediate action, phases should and will be bypassed.

GREAT PARENT CONFERENCES

Be Prepared!

Educators want to be confident and prepared for all parent meetings. Never go into any meeting, and especially a parent meeting, appearing confused and not sure of what is going on. Do not give the impression that you have not discussed the issues with the other teachers and that you do not know what is going on in the other classes. The parent meeting should not be the place where a teacher first hears what a student is doing in the other classes.

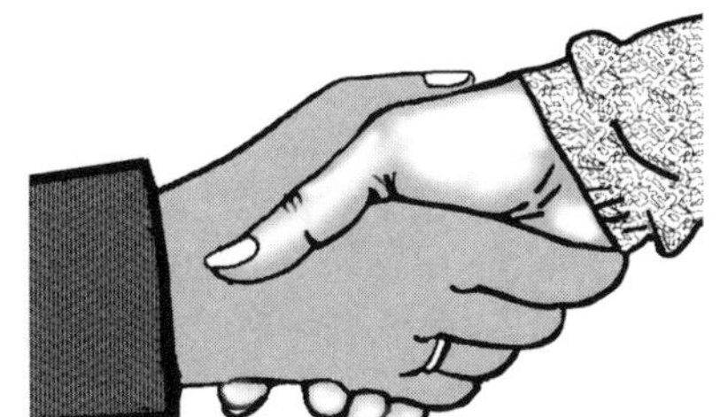

All too often, I have heard teachers say things in parent conferences like, "This is what he is doing in my class. I do not know what he is doing in any of the other classes."

Meet as a team to make sure everyone is on the same page before a parent meeting. A couple of minutes of preparation can make all the difference between a productive conference with parents and one that is not. No teacher, counselor, or administrator should ever bring up something during the parent meeting that was not shared in the preparation meeting. Five minutes spent as a team getting ready for the parent conference can save 20 minutes at the actual conference. Agree on ground rules for conferences before the meetings take place. You will want to consider adopting the two basic guidelines explained below:

#1 Do not use any teacher's personal name in reference to his or her class, including your own. With the exception of initial introductions, name the subject, not the teacher's name, when referencing a class.

When we use teachers' names in reference to classes, the issues are always personal. When we reference the classes by the subject name, the process is more professional.

For example, for an imagined conference, the teachers are Mr. Browder for Math, Mrs. Smith for social studies, Mrs. Miller for science, and Mr. Walker for language arts. Mr. Thompson is the administrator for this meeting, and Mrs. Dropkick is the counselor.

After the initial introductions, the team will not refer to what is happening in Mrs. Miller's class, but will always reference what is happening in the science class. For example, Do not say, "Mrs. Miller is not the one that does not allow gum chewing in the class." Do say, "The safety requirements of science prohibit gum chewing." Even when talking about your own classes, reference them in the third person as much as possible. Use the class name instead of talking about "my class." This will keep the meeting from getting personal.

Students and parents often talk about perceived personality conflicts, when the actual conflict is with the subject matter and not with the teacher. When we avoid saying that Mr. Browder requires a certain amount of homework, and we talk instead about requirements of the math curriculum, we focus on the class and the work, not the teacher.

Always talk about a student's behavior in reference to how the behavior affects his or her learning. Do not reference how the behavior affects anyone else, or the class.

Educators need to emphasize how disruptive the student is; however, as soon as they start in on the problems and burdens one student is putting on others in the class, the parents of that one student are put on the defensive. It is a simple fact that people cannot listen very well when they feel they have to defend themselves.

We want, and need, the parents to be good listeners, so we have to do everything we can to help them be able to listen to what we have to share with them. While it would be accurate to describe Rodney's inappropriate behavior by stating, "Rodney is disrupting the rest of the class when he turns around or gets out of his seat and speaks out of turn. I simply cannot teach the rest of the students when Rodney is acting out." Consider saying instead something like, "Rodney cannot pay attention, and I really can't teach him when he turns around, gets out of his seat, and speaks out of turn. I need Rodney's attention if I am going to help him be successful in math."

You address the same behaviors, but you emphasize how the behaviors are limiting Rodney's ability to learn and be successful in your classroom. In the first example, parents will be on the defensive, and you have opened the door to what Rodney has been telling his parents about other students. Everyone knows that if Rodney is distracting himself in the manners described, he is probably also distracting others in the process. Since we have talked about wanting Rodney not to be a distraction to himself, we keep the focus on him, which, by the way, is the reason his parents are there.

Step-by-Step to Successful Parent/Team Meetings

Legendary coach John Wooden is quoted as saying "Failure to prepare is preparing to fail!" There are a few things teams should always discuss prior to the parent meeting, even if it is just the five minutes before the meeting. It does not take very long to be very prepared for the meeting. The following strategies will make for successful team/parent meetings.

Step One: Decide who will facilitate the meeting.

We often get to the table and are not sure who is going to speak first. There should be a person who is clearly the facilitator for the meeting. If you are meeting as a team with the parent, and the facilitator is one of the teachers, the facilitator should be the one that is having the most success with the student; sometimes, this will be a counselor or an administrator. Keep the meeting as positive as possible. Start with a positive comment about the student, if at all possible.

Step Two: Identify key issues.

As a team, find out what is going on with the student. By the time there is the need for a parent meeting, there are often multiple issues to try to deal with. It is important to get everything out on the table when the meeting involves staff only. A teacher should never bring up something at the conference that was not put on the table during the planning session. This way, the facilitator can summarize quickly what the team sees as the issues.

Step Three: Determine as a group the key issue for this conference.

Come to the meeting able to summarize the issues and have one key issue to discuss in detail with the parents. Select something to tackle with the parents that the team feels could end successfully. Choose an issue the parents, the student, and the teachers can all focus on.

Step Four: Provide a concrete suggestion for the parents that will help resolve this issue.

Remember Rodney? Let's say in his case the team decided that the key issue was Rodney's lack of preparation for class. Rodney never has his homework or books and materials for class; therefore, he cannot participate as teachers review homework or work from the previous day. That is the time Rodney gets off task, and it goes downhill from there. So your suggestion as a team is to have Rodney take his planner home each night and have his parents sign it indicating that Rodney has done his homework and will be prepared for his classes. Teachers each period will make sure Rodney has his books and materials for whatever class follows theirs.

Step Five: Decide who will follow up with the parent and when that follow-up will occur.

It is critical that every parent conference of any type has a follow-up contact. So during the planning for the conference, someone on the team should volunteer to do the follow-up contact with the parents. In Rodney's case, one team member will call his parents sometime after the meeting to let them know if teachers are actually receiving the signed agenda book and if Rodney is arriving more prepared than before. As the meeting is coming to a close, the teacher that volunteers to do the follow-up will speak to Rodney's parents, stating something such as "Thank you all for coming. I think helping Rodney be more prepared for class by getting his homework done will be a great help for Rodney. I will give you a call next week to let you know if he is bringing in his agenda book and homework each day. What day and time would be best for me to give you a call?"

By the way, the same "always follow up" rule pertains to calling parents. Never call a parent just once. Always end the phone conversation by setting up a time for a follow-up conversation. As the phone call or the parent meeting is coming to a close, you should always finish with "Thank you for your time and I will call you next Thursday to let you know how it is going and if there has been the improvement that we are all hoping for." Major companies call customers and ask about their satisfaction after something is delivered and installed. This is not only "good business," but it also ensures that the parents follow up on their end because they know you are going to call back soon.

A Scenario for a Successful Parent Meeting

The team is now ready for the parent conference, and the preplanning helps you and your teammates feel confident. Rodney's parents arrive and are taken to the team planning area. Someone from the team escorts them to the team or conference room. The seating arrangement is casual. Everyone sits around a table or in an area with some of the teachers beside the parents as well as in front of them. Parents are offered a small selection of beverages and some cookies as they take their seats. The team has made the parents feel as comfortable as possible.

The facilitator welcomes Rodney's parents and thanks them for coming. She introduces everyone at the table by name and subject. Remember, this is the last time any of the staff at the meeting will use any of the teachers' personal names. The facilitator continues by saying something positive about Rodney, and goes on to explain to the parents that the team has several issues concerning Rodney's behavior and academic performance. She explains that in preparing for this meeting the team has looked at the issues, which she summarizes, and then she shares that the team has decided that they would like to focus on one primary issue. She says, "The team believes focusing on this one issue will have a positive impact on Rodney's behavior and academic performance in general." The facilitator clearly states the key issue: helping Rodney arrive prepared for school and class.

The facilitator continues to explain that when Rodney does not have his homework, he is not able to take part as class begins, and he gets distracted. So the team would like to help Rodney make sure he has his homework and is ready for each of his classes. The facilitator shows the parents Rodney's agenda book and explains that in the agenda book, they will see Rodney's assignments. The facilitator shows the parents the place they can sign to indicate that Rodney has taken his agenda book home. The facilitator says, "We would like for one of you to check on Rodney's work and sign the book each night. We will check it in the morning. We will also take a few minutes at the end of each period to make sure Rodney has the books and materials he needs for the next class."

The facilitator finishes by telling the parents that the team believes that if Rodney is better prepared for class many other issues that distract Rodney from his learning would be resolved. The facilitator asks Rodney's parents if they have additional suggestions for helping Rodney be better prepared for his classes, and if they agree with the team's suggestions.

This introduction by the facilitator does not take very long. However, the facilitator has given the meeting direction and has charted a course for the meeting while setting a positive solution-oriented tone for the meeting. The first time the parents speak, they are already talking about solutions to help their child. The parents have not had to be defensive. Many times you will see how parents begin to relax.

Many parents are amazed by how painless conferences with professional, well-prepared teachers can be. Of course, your team will have the times where the parent came to get his or her pound of flesh, and have not had their chance to tear into any of the teachers. So, when given the chance to talk, they start to vent their frustrations. The facilitator should say something like, "We know how frustrated you are, and we know you want the best for your child." An additional statement should focus the parents back to the key issue. Since the facilitator established the primary focus in the introduction, it is easier to refocus the parents back to that point. If the team does not establish a point of focus early, the meeting can wander all over the place.

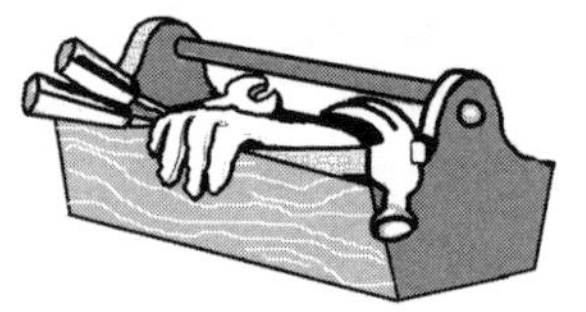

Tools for Successful Parent Conferences

Mark Twain said "If the only tool you have is a hammer, then everything looks like a nail." Here are a few tools for less stressful and more productive parent-team conferences. These tools simply require a little common sense mixed with southern hospitality.

- Before you say anything to anyone, ask yourself three questions:
  Is it true?
  Is it kind?
  Is it necessary?
- Have some refreshments available.
- Avoid the words "never" and "always" when describing an issue to a parent.
- Do not make statements such as "I've done all that I can do . . ." or "I've tried everything", because you haven't yet. You wouldn't want your doctor to throw in the towel. Teachers must come to every meeting with the idea that there is something out there that is going to work.
- Focus on issues, not personalities. Do not take personally things parents say to you, and do not get personal. If parents use a teacher's name, remember to use the subject name in response.
- Be an active listener! *(I sat in on one parent-team meeting recently in which one of the teachers was eating, one was over at her computer, and two were having a side conversation while the parent was talking to the one teacher paying attention.)*
- Paraphrase the parents' statements to show empathy. Each time it is your turn to speak, try to start with, "I understand what you mean about . . . ," "I hear what you're saying . . . ," or best yet, "You are correct about . . . ," and then continue with your part of the conversation.
- Maintain good eye contact and remember that you are always communicating, so be very aware of your body language and remember that nodding affirmatively does not necessarily indicate agreement, but rather acknowledgement.
- Do not make conditions you cannot enforce. Do not say things such as "He cannot come back to my class unless . . . ."

- Do not threaten or intimidate—ever.
- Take ownership of the problem. In your strategy, state what you are going to do differently to help address the problem as well as what you want the child to do differently. This is where you are going to use the pronoun "I."
- You are the ultimate salesperson, and you really want/need to make this sale! "I want this to work out . . . ," "I am willing to try . . . ," "I want your child to be successful in math, so . . . ."
- Remember, you cannot change another person's behavior without changing your own!
- No one can change or affect your attitude, unless you allow them to do so.

TAG . . . You're It!

Parent-Teacher Teams

Schedule one or more parent-team conferences, and use the conferences for these exercises.

Exercise One

Select a few students that may be in line for future parent-team conferences. Go through the planning process for the upcoming parent-team conference. The form on page 144 is an example of one team's organizer for planning.

Exercise Two

After planning for the parent-team conference, facilitate a successful parent-team conference following the step-by-step process. Your team might even try a dry run of the conference with someone like the counselor or an administrator playing the part of the parents.

Exercise Three

Process the conference and self-assess the team's performance. The team can use the step-by-step strategies (pages 137 and 138) as a checklist to evaluate the conference. Identify things the team did well, and discuss what adjustments the team will need to make for the next conference. Each parent-team conference is an opportunity for the team to monitor and adjust its performance.

______________________Conference Form

Conference: ____ Team/Student ____ Team/Parent ____ Team/Student/Parent

Student's Name: ______________________ Date: ____________

Faculty Present: ______________________

____

____

Areas needing improvement: ______________________

____

Content Area Analysis by Individual Teachers:

Read/Write: ______________________

____

____

Math: ______________________

____

____

Science: ______________________

____

____

Social Studies: ______________________

____

____

Other: ______________________

____

____

Recommended adjustments to enhance student performance/achievement:

1. ______________________
____

2. ______________________
____

3. ______________________
____

4. ______________________
____

3. ______________________
____

Follow-up visit: ___ yes ___ no   Date scheduled: ____________

Parent/Guardian Signature/Date: ______________________

Student Signature/Date: ______________________

Please Join the Jackson Middle School 7th Grade Teachers

Spring Conference

March 24 - 25, 2009

Parents,

This has been an exciting year of growth for your seventh grader. Our upcoming Spring Conference gives us an opportunity to share your child's academic progress with you, and discuss our team goals for the remainder of the school year. We look forward to meeting with you on Tuesday the 24th, or Wednesday the 25th, at 3:00 p.m. in the school cafeteria.

The 7th Grade Teachers

One team sends out invitations to their parents for parent-teacher/team conferences!

Flexing the Team Schedule

Improving the Team's Flexibility

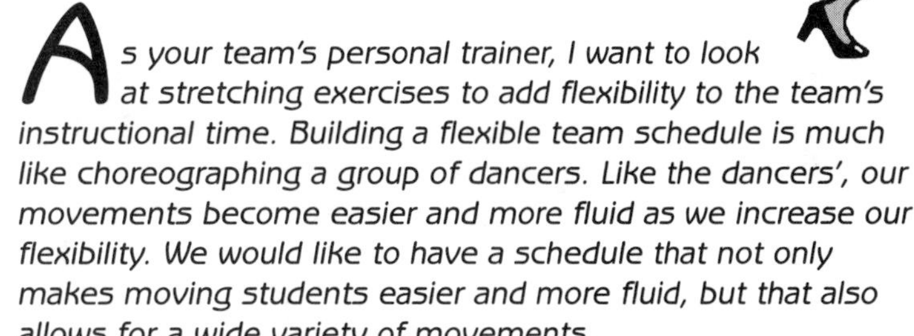

As your team's personal trainer, I want to look at stretching exercises to add flexibility to the team's instructional time. Building a flexible team schedule is much like choreographing a group of dancers. Like the dancers', our movements become easier and more fluid as we increase our flexibility. We would like to have a schedule that not only makes moving students easier and more fluid, but that also allows for a wide variety of movements.

The schedule is critical in determining how instruction will be delivered. A schedule that is too tight restricts opportunities for teachers on a team to implement instructional strategies such as flexible student groupings, rotating classes, integrating the curriculum, and giving common assessments and authentic assessments.

We are going to do "yoga" with your team schedule, and help make it as limber as possible. We may not get to the "Cirque de Soleil" level of contortion, but your team should at least be able touch its toes.

For teams to flex their schedules they need a flexible block schedule and they must make scheduling a regular team meeting consideration. When the team dedicates planning time to the process, and the teachers consider new possibilities each time they meet, then they will become more flexible with their instructional time. As with many other teaming strategies, this process will require communication, collaboration, and especially open minds. This process also requires understanding the learning needs of the students. Educators should not alter schedules just to do it. Flexing the schedule should be done only to meet the instructional needs of the students.

Flexing the Team Schedule Requires

* Team Planning Time
* Collaboration
* Communication
* Understanding the Needs of Students
* Open Minds

What Is a Flexible Schedule?

A school has a flexible schedule if teams can:

- change the length of classes;
- change the order of classes; and
- change the student groupings

Flex the Schedule: Change the Length of Classes

The team should be able to change the length of its classes. If class periods are usually 50 minutes, each the team should be able to take ten minutes off each period and run 40-minute periods to accommodate a team activity. Teams might change the length of classes to show a demonstration video, screen an appropriate movie, or allow a guest speaker to address the entire team at one time.

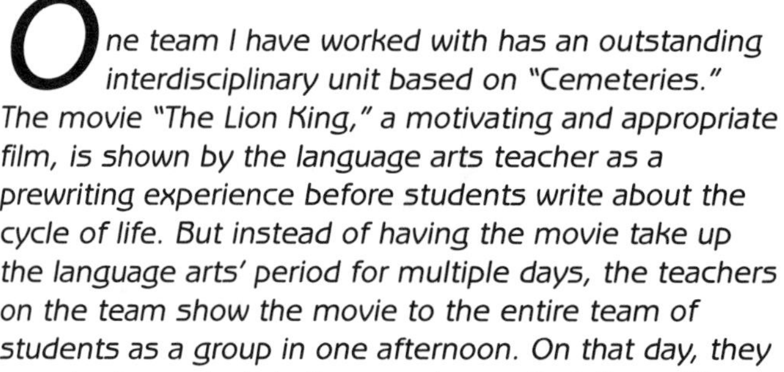
One team I have worked with has an outstanding interdisciplinary unit based on "Cemeteries." The movie "The Lion King," a motivating and appropriate film, is shown by the language arts teacher as a prewriting experience before students write about the cycle of life. But instead of having the movie take up the language arts' period for multiple days, the teachers on the team show the movie to the entire team of students as a group in one afternoon. On that day, they run shorter periods in the morning so that they still see all of their students.

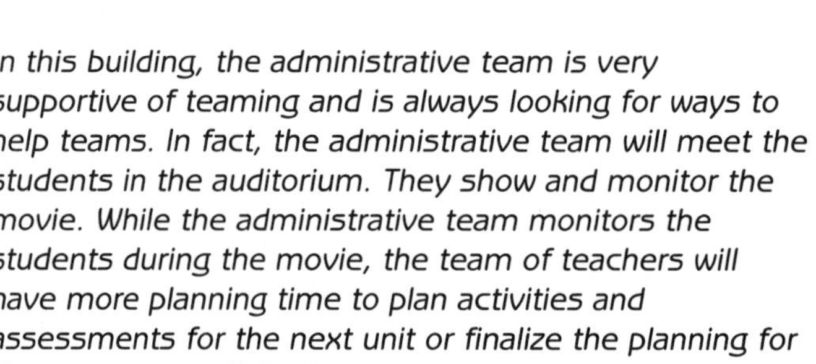
In this building, the administrative team is very supportive of teaming and is always looking for ways to help teams. In fact, the administrative team will meet the students in the auditorium. They show and monitor the movie. While the administrative team monitors the students during the movie, the team of teachers will have more planning time to plan activities and assessments for the next unit or finalize the planning for the current unit. Talk about a great use of time!

The schedule below shows how the whole team can view a movie or hear a speaker at the same time when the length of each class is changed. The teachers still plan to see all of their students during the morning. (They will run 35-minute periods.) Then all eighth graders will see the movie after lunch. In this case, the students will go from the movie to their exploratory classes. Since the administrative team is going to show the movie for the team, this means the teachers can have the time from lunch to dismissal for planning. *(An administrative team can often help teams make the most of their time.)*

<table>
<tr><th></th><th>5th Grade</th><th>6th Grade</th><th>7th Grade</th><th>8th Grade</th></tr>
<tr><td rowspan="2">1</td><td rowspan="5">Exploratory Block
Core Team Planning</td><td rowspan="9">Core
BLOCK</td><td rowspan="6">Core
BLOCK</td><td rowspan="10">Periods will be 35 minutes instead of 50 minutes.</td></tr>
<tr></tr>
<tr><td rowspan="2">2</td></tr>
<tr></tr>
<tr><td rowspan="2">3</td></tr>
<tr><td rowspan="6">Core
BLOCK</td></tr>
<tr><td rowspan="2">4</td><td rowspan="4">Exploratory Block
Core Team Planning</td></tr>
<tr></tr>
<tr><td rowspan="2">5</td></tr>
<tr><td rowspan="2">Exploratory Block
Core Team Planning</td></tr>
<tr><td rowspan="2"></td><td>LUNCH</td><td>LUNCH</td></tr>
<tr><td>LUNCH</td><td>LUNCH</td><td rowspan="7">Core
BLOCK</td><td rowspan="3">Admin Team shows movie during this part of the core block.</td></tr>
<tr><td rowspan="2">6</td><td rowspan="6">Core
BLOCK</td><td rowspan="2">Exploratory Block
Core Team Planning</td></tr>
<tr></tr>
<tr><td rowspan="2">7</td><td rowspan="4">Core
BLOCK</td><td rowspan="4">Exploratory Block
Core Team Planning</td></tr>
<tr></tr>
<tr><td rowspan="2">8</td></tr>
<tr></tr>
</table>

Flex the Schedule: Change the Order of Classes

The team should be able to flex (change the order or rotate) its classes. Flexing a schedule to administer a common assessment is a good example of how this change is advantageous to both students and teachers. Many teams give most of their assessments as common assessments. This might mean that the entire team gives the upcoming social studies assessment at the same time so that all students are taking the assessment the first period in the core block. Not only is this more brain appropriate, but since state assessments are administered as common assessments, students will practice and become more comfortable with this format throughout the school year. The following paragraphs discuss some appropriate reasons to flex the team schedule by changing the order of classes.

 ***Reason #1***

Setting Up a Common Assessment

One of the questions that the teachers on the team should ask weekly is if any teacher is going to be giving an assessment. If the answer is yes, ask:

- Can the assessment be given as a common assessment?
- Is it an authentic assessment?

When one teacher gives assessments in the usual way, the teacher administers the assessment each period all day. In this format, teachers limit students' learning opportunities for all students except those who took the assessment during the first hour. In the first period, some students are taking the assessment while the rest of the students are trying to learn new material in the other classes. Students in the other classes will be taking the assessment sometime later in the day. As they try to learn new information, their brains are busy trying to keep the information ready for the upcoming assessment. It is much more difficult for these students to give their full attention to new material while they are thinking about the assessment.

In the second period and beyond, the situation only gets worse. While some of the students are taking the assessment, all of the other classes have a mix of students—some of the students will have completed the assessment, while others will still be waiting to take the assessment.

Every teacher on the planet knows what these students are doing. They are, of course, discussing the assessment with each other. By the way, I don't consider this discussion cheating. I would call it cooperative learning!

The distractions for the teachers not giving the assessment get progressively worse as the day goes on. To avoid this situation, the team should work together and flex the schedule. All of the teachers on the team can administer the assessment first thing in the block, and then the team will begin period one after the assessment. All of the teachers will have to give up a few minutes from each of their periods, but they will not have distracted learners. The students will all be done with the assessment and they will be better able to focus on their other classes. In addition, the teacher who "owns" the assessment gives it once in the morning with the rest of the team, and then is able to move into valuable post-assessment activities with students for the remainder of the day.

Reason #2
Developing Assessment Modifications

It can be difficult for teachers to make adaptations and modifications to assessments for individual students when assessments are given in the traditional manner. For example, some students benefit from having the assessment read to them and some benefit from doing only a portion of an assessment. For a teacher doing multiple modifications, every period is very difficult at best. Assessment adaptations and modifications are rare unless there is a separate class for special needs students with IEPs.

Many students in addition to those specified with IEPs would benefit from assessment adaptations and modifications. When the team helps administer the assessment, this becomes a nonissue. Adaptations and modifications for assessments are possible for more students. A teacher simply assigns each student to a room according to the adaptation and modification being made. In one room, the test is read aloud; in another room, students do only a portion of the assessment.

Calculate the length of the classes based on the length of the assessment. The longer the assessment is, the shorter the classes will be—which means that the shorter the assessment is, the longer the periods will be. Remember my dad's military acronym "KISS" (Keep It Simple Stupid) when choosing a method for doing things. I am often impressed how the simplest of adaptations to the team schedule can have such a meaningful impact on student performance.

The first row indicates the class period. The second row indicates the regular schedule for the team. The third row reflects what the schedule will look like on the day of the team common assessment or an authentic assessment.

Period 1 2 3 4 5 6 7

<table>
<tr><td colspan="2">Core Classes
55 minutes with five-minute passing</td><td>Exploratory Classes</td></tr>
<tr><td>Common Assessment
60 minutes</td><td>1 2 3 4 5
Core Classes 48 minutes</td><td>6 7
Exploratory Classes</td></tr>
</table>

 ***Reason #3***

Setting Up an Authentic Assessment

The science teacher is beginning the unit on biomes. The teacher gives students six ways to demonstrate their knowledge of each biome. For each biome, the students may choose between making a collage, doing drawings or paintings, building a physical model, acting as a reporter broadcasting from the biome to tell about the biome *(Students might read their scripts for the teacher or use a tape recorder.)*, writing a short story or skit that takes place in the biome, or writing a song about the biome. The teacher demonstrates and goes over the grading rubric for each assessment option with the students. Since these are formative assessments, students will be creating products as they learn about each of the biomes.

For this unit, rubrics are built only on the products, and not on the presentations. The students know the grade that they have earned before they present their projects. This alleviates much of the student apprehension since they do not have to worry about the grade as part of the presentation.

For the collage, the students will collect pictures and label the pictures with the teacher as they progress. The teacher and the student negotiate and agree on the grade the student will receive prior to the student presenting the collage. Only when the student gets the collage to a level of quality that both the teacher and student agree on will the student present his or her collage. On assessment day, the students present their collages.

Student reporters "broadcasting" from the various biomes will be creating their scripts as they go through the lessons. On assessment day, they read their final script that the teacher has approved. The student songwriters have picked their melodies and added their lyrics as they studied the biomes. On assessment day, they share or record their masterpieces.

Some of the students will opt to write a short story or skit that is built around the biomes. The students will share their stories with the teacher as they go through the unit, indicating where in the story or skit they are describing the biome.

One student wrote an "Indiana Jones" type adventure; she described each of the biomes quite well as her hero traveled the globe to save the world from imminent destruction.

As the assessment day approaches, the science teacher talks with the team about the assessment sharing. The teacher divides the students into five groups. Each of the teachers on the team will host one group. So, a couple of the teachers will have the students presenting the collages or their drawings and paintings. The science teacher might have the students with the physical models, as that is sometimes messy. The students that have chosen to be the reporters, songwriters, and authors will go to other rooms. Of course, the team can choose to mix and match the assessment types.

Students will be able to switch between assessment types throughout the unit and not have to be reporter for the entire unit. A student may choose to do the first biome as a reporter and the second as an artist.

Having students make a variety of presentations can be very time-consuming. However, when the entire team shares the responsibility, it actually is quite simple. In 30 minutes, the science teacher might be able to have five or six students present their finished product. With the team's help, that number jumps to 25 or 30 students. With a few days a week, the team has dramatically changed the assessment process.

Authentic and formative assessments are powerful tools, but they are labor-intensive and time-consuming for the teacher trying to implement them. Each assessment requires a variety of assessment formats, rubrics, and evaluations. I suggest that each teacher on the team try to develop one authentic assessment per year. That way, students receive the benefits of authentic assessments several times a year, but each teacher has to create only one assessment.

☆ *Reason #4*
Making the Authentic Assessment Work

Suppose each teacher on the team teaches five of the seven daily periods as shown below, and each of the periods is fifty-five minutes long, with five minutes of passing time between each period. This gives the teachers 300 minutes of flexible time, including the class and passing times.

The first row shows a regular day with students going to exploratory classes during periods six and seven. Teachers take 30 minutes for the assessment first thing in the block for several days. That will leave them with 270 minutes for five periods and passing times (270 ÷ 5 = 54). Therefore, classes will be 54 minutes minus the passing. If five minutes is designated for passing, the classes will be 49 minutes each.

The second row reflects the different schedule for students on that day. Notice that whatever the team does with their time in the core block, the time to go to exploratory classes does not change.

☆ *Reason #5*
Creating Extended Learning Time

How can a team create **extended learning time** for their classes? The easiest example of this is a schedule where teachers teach six periods in an eight-period school day. Teachers see half of their classes on one day (the A day) and the other half of their students on the next day (the B day). In a traditional eight-period schedule, with 45-minute classes and three-minute passing periods, the core teachers would have six 45-minute periods each day. In an A-B schedule, the teachers would teach three 95-minute classes each day.

Regular Schedule		A-B Schedule
Periods are 45 minutes long.		Periods are 95 minutes long.
Monday	1-2-3-4-5-6	A day 1-2-3
Tuesday	1-2-3-4-5-6	B day 4-5-6
Wednesday	1-2-3-4-5-6	A day 1-2-3
Thursday	1-2-3-4-5-6	B day 4-5-6
Friday	1-2-3-4-5-6	A day 1-2-3
Monday	1-2-3-4-5-6	B day 4-5-6

Note that teachers see students three times one week, then two times the following week. Half of the passing times are eliminated and all of that time goes into instruction. Hallway issues are also cut in half. Teachers grade half as many papers each day, and students have half as much work to do each day.

Creating an A-B schedule is easy when teachers teach an even number of periods, but I promised you extreme flexibility! What if teachers teach five periods instead of six? In this instance teachers have 48-minute periods with a three-minute passing time. That means the

core block is a total of 255 minutes long. Simply divide the core block into three periods instead of five. Dividing the time by three instead of five increases the instructional time for each block. Each teacher sees each class for three 81-minute periods per week.

When teachers see three groups of students a day instead of five, they eliminate two passing times, and the time gained goes directly into instructional time. This is often called a **modified block** and translates into extra instructional time. Teachers have less "administrivia" like taking roll and passing out materials. The schedule below shows a schedule for extended learning time for teachers teaching five periods a day. This is a very popular schedule for teachers wanting more instructional time.

Modified Block

Benefits include:

- Increased instructional time
- Some passing time goes into instruction
- Teachers can use more instructional strategies
- Students spend less time in the hallways
- Fewer papers for teachers to grade daily
- Fewer assignments for students per day

DAY	PERIOD
Mon	1-2-3
Tue	4-5-1
Wed	2-3-4
Thu	5-1-2
Fri	3-4-5

The teachers rotate their periods seeing each class three times each week. The three periods a day are 81 minutes each with a three-minute passing period.

☆ *Reason #6*
Rotating the Order of Classes

Students and teachers perform differently at various parts of the day. In most schedules, whichever classes a student has just before lunch or during the last period of the day are locked in at least for a semester and, most often, for the entire year. These periods are not generally the most productive times of the day for teachers or students.

In a flexible schedule, a class is not locked into a particular period. The team can rotate the classes to keep any one class from the same difficult, or for that matter, prime time of the day. For each student and teacher, the prime time of the day may be different. Teachers should get to see all students, and students should get to see all their teachers in their best time of the day.

Rotating the schedule is actually one of the easiest things a team can do, and every team I have worked with that has tried it has reported amazing results. Teachers share how differently some students are at different times of the day. Some students have difficulties getting to school on time. If the team rotates their schedule, the student is not always late to the same class.

Students have shared with me how different teachers are when they get to see them at different times of the day. This is an actual quote from one young man:

> "You know, Mister, Mrs. ____ is not so bad in the afternoon after she has had some coffee and she's been fed!" His team was just beginning to try rotating their schedule, and he was on his way to the last period class. This was the teacher that he had for first period before the rotation.

Now, I am not sure if he was different or if his teacher was different after coffee and food. Either way, they were seeing each other differently and they were not locked into one time of the day. The following schedule shows rotation of classes in a modified block schedule. They rotate each week, so the team would be in a schedule for one week and then they would shift to the next part of the rotation the next week. In the weekly rotation, five of seven classes meet each day, so they complete the rotations to get back to where they started in six weeks. Both examples are included here.

Rotating Schedules

Daily Rotation		*Weekly Rotation*	
DAY	PERIOD	WEEK	PERIOD
Mon	1-2-3-4-5	week 1	1-2-3-4-5
Tue	2-3-4-5-1	week 2	2-3-4-5-1
Wed	3-4-5-1-2	week 3	3-4-5-1-2
Thu	4-5-1-2-3	week 4	4-5-1-2-3
Fri	5-1-2-3-4	week 5	5-1-2-3-4
Mon	1-2-3-4-5	week 6	1-2-3-4-5

Reason #7

Adding a Class for Enrichment or Other Special Situations: The Rotating Drop Schedule

Sometimes teams add enrichment experiences for the students that are not provided in the regular curriculum. For example:

- the team may want to add some review opportunities for the state assessment for a few days or weeks prior to the state test;
- the team may want to have the students write and practice skits that the students will perform for the parents at the next open house;
- the team may want to have the students do a Civil War reenactment with the help of some community members that participate in reenactments around the country; or
- the team may want to have the students participate in challenge course problem-solving initiative activities.

There are two common elements to all of these activities. First, they are all curriculum-based activities that enhance the standard curriculum. Secondly, they are all short-term activities (at most, a few weeks in duration). So the question is, how can the team accommodate these curriculum-based activities without giving up a few weeks of the regular curriculum?

Teams can use a **rotating drop schedule** to solve this dilemma. The team simply adds a new class to the rotation. If the teachers teach five of seven periods as described above, then they are going put a sixth period into the rotation. That sixth period will be the period that accommodates the curriculum-based activity. The team will have to decide what each of the teachers will be doing regarding the new experience and then assign the students accordingly. For example, the students might be distributed by their groups determined as a part of their science classes. Each teacher on the team will be assigned four of the skit groups, and the groups will work on their skits in the new period the team has created.

Since the students are accustomed to a rotating schedule, the teachers simply explain that they are adding a new class to the regular rotation. The teachers explain what students are going to be doing in the new class. Of course, once the rotation has been established, the teachers can move students between classes for the new period. For example, if the team is doing a play, a student may be a stagehand in the first act of the play, and an actor in the second act. The teachers are able to move the students around in the new class as needed.

With six classes now in the rotation, and only five periods for the classes to fit in, one class drops out each day. On the first day, the students will go to periods one through five as usual. The teachers tell the students that the next day they will begin with period two, as usual. However, they will report to the new class last period instead of period one. That means the next day, students will go to classes two through six (the new class). Period one is dropped from the rotation for the day.

Every day, or each week depending on the rotation, one period is dropped from the schedule to accommodate the new class. That means that five out of every six days the teachers see their regular students in their regular classes. However, the teachers now see the students five out of every six days in the new curriculum-based experience the teachers have designed to supplement the regular curriculum. This is an effective and efficient way to add invaluable experiences to the curriculum. Sometimes all of the teachers are focused on one experience, like the skits, and sometimes each teacher will offer something different. When the teachers offer a variety of experiences in the extra period, the extra classes the team creates are often referred to as a "core wheel."

Rotating Drop Schedules

Daily Rotation			*Weekly Rotation*		
DAY	PERIOD	PERIOD DROPPED	WEEK	PERIOD	PERIOD DROPPED
Mon	1-2-3-4-5	6	week 1	1-2-3-4-5	6
Tue	2-3-4-5-6	1	week 2	2-3-4-5-6	1
Wed	3-4-5-6-1	2	week 3	3-4-5-6-1	2
Thu	4-5-6-1-2	3	week 4	4-5-6-1-2	3
Fri	5-6-1-2-3	4	week 5	5-6-1-2-3	4
Mon	6-1-2-3-4	5	week 6	6-1-2-3-4	5

Flex the Schedule: Change the Student Groupings

The team should be able to change the student groupings between classes to accommodate both academic and disciplinary issues. Occasionally, teachers use student groups to implement instructional strategies. One example is in science class when students are working in lab groups. Another is explained in the chapter on Curriculum Development where a math teacher puts students into groups representing fictitious "construction companies" for a bid project. As the project develops, other teachers assign work for the "companies." For a few days each marking period, the team creates a schedule where the students move through their day as "construction companies." It makes perfect sense for the students to travel in these groups for a few days to work on the environmental policy for their construction company in science. (See the chapter on Curriculum Development for the details of the interdisciplinary unit.)

Sometimes, teachers see the need for changing students between classes for social or other academic reasons. *(However, teachers often tell me that it can take an act of Congress to get a student's schedule changed.)*

Utilizing teams, this is a very simple task. In fact, since the students will always have the same teachers for their core classes, moving students between and among classes is really a period change and nothing more.

Flexing the Block

Teams should make flexing the schedule a weekly team-meeting topic. As the team becomes more sophisticated in scheduling techniques, they will look at other considerations; however, the basic questions the teams should ask at every team meeting where the schedule is the topic are:

- Does anyone have an assessment coming up?
  How can the team assist with the assessment?
- Do any of the teachers need to add any curriculum-based activities that might not fit into the regular schedule?
- Is anyone doing any group activities?
  Will it be helpful for the groups to be working together later in the other classes?
  Is there a multi-disciplinary project involved?
- Do we have any team activities coming up?
  Team celebrations, field trips
- Are there any school-sponsored activities we need to plan around?
  It helps to preplan for schoolwide activities like speakers and pep rallies.
- Do any of the teachers have any speakers coming in?
- Are any of the teachers showing a video to all of the classes?
- Are there any other considerations for next week's schedule and beyond?

Combining the Flexes

As teams work at the three ways to flex their team schedules, they will see opportunities for combining one or more of the three. One example was really already listed as teachers changed the length of their classes for the common assessment, and regrouped students at the same time for assessment adaptations and modifications. Another example is creating the rotation to change the order of the classes in combination with changing the length of the classes in the modified block. The only limit to the number of ways for the team to flex its schedule is the imagination of the teachers on the team. *(Knowing teachers as I do, I would say that the sky is the limit!)*

TAG . . . You're It!

Flexing

Exercise One

I recommend that teams make flexing their schedule a weekly topic, and look for ways that they can enhance instruction by flexing the instructional time. If your team is already in a flexible block schedule, you will, of course, want to use your own schedule.

A. Work with your teammates to design a schedule that will accommodate a guest speaker that is available for only one hour during the day. (You pick the hour.) Math and writing assignments due that day make it necessary for every teacher to see every student.

B. Your team is doing a mock trial and science labs this week, and both activities could benefit from longer classes. Develop an A-B or a modified block schedule increasing the length of all classes.

Exercise Two

I recommend that teams make the school's master schedule a monthly topic during team time. Think about what is working and what suggestions you might make to improve the schedule for next year. In this exercise, look at your school's schedule and determine if the schedule maximizes the instructional blocks. What suggestions would you make to put more flexibility in the schedule?

Inclusion on the Team

Double-Teaming To Meet The Needs Of All Students

As the team's personal trainer, I want to explain how having a special needs teacher on the team not only meets the needs of the special needs students, but also benefits every student on the team. The strategies presented in this chapter show how having a special needs teacher assigned to a team strengthens the team. There are many things the regular education and special education teachers can do to enhance the learning environment for every student in an inclusion classroom.

Some of the terms in this chapter are used in different ways throughout the educational community. Please note definitions of the following words:

- **inclusion**
  I will use the term *inclusion* to indicate a situation in which special needs students are included in regular education classes where a special needs teacher is coteaching with a regular education teacher. Inclusion means that the special needs teacher is physically present in the regular education classroom with a regular education teacher. The regular and special needs teachers share equally the instructional and assessment responsibilities for all of the students in the class.

- **mainstream**
  When special needs students are in regular education classes with only the regular education teacher, I will use the term *mainstream*. When special needs students are mainstreamed, the special needs teachers usually act as teacher consultants. As teacher consultants, the special needs teachers suggest strategies and modifications for the regular education teachers to use when they work with the special needs students. The special needs teacher is not actually present in the regular education classroom.

- **pullout**
  When the special needs teacher teaches only special needs students in a separate group, I will use the term *pullout*.

Maximizing the Possibilities

> *"We should not only use the brains that we have, but all that we can borrow."*
> – *Woodrow Wilson*

Whenever possible, a special needs teacher with his or her caseload should be assigned to only one team. Special needs teachers may be assigned to multiple teams. Special needs teachers can attend one team meeting and meet the needs of many special needs students assigned to that team rather than try to find the teachers individually. Unfortunately, staffing may not always allow this.

Having special needs teachers work with multiple teams is considerably less efficient and effective, but it is infinitely better than the random scheduling with no team assignments. If a special needs teacher has students assigned to three teams, he or she can talk to all of the core teachers from the three teams by attending three meetings. Without teams, the special needs teacher may have to schedule as many as fifteen separate meetings to talk with core teachers.

The ultimate goal for scheduling special needs teachers should be that each teacher is assigned to one team, and every effort should be made to achieve this goal.

Each team should reflect the overall student population with a proportional number of high-, middle-, and low-performing students. However, one type of high-, middle-, and low-performing students may be placed on a single team to centralize the services provided by a teacher or teachers serving that population. For example, one team may have special needs students; one team, 504 students; another, speech, language, and ESL students; and another, other identified at-risk students.

When special needs teachers work with multiple teams, consultative support is challenging, but "accomplishable." The situation creates serious problems for *inclusion*. It becomes very difficult for the special needs teacher to get to multiple team meetings and adequately plan with other teachers for instruction in cotaught classes. When special needs teachers are not able to attend team meetings, the teams have to make special efforts to communicate with them. In this case, one member of the team should volunteer to be the liaison with the special needs teacher and communicate what happens at each team meeting. When inclusion is involved, a caring administrator will also provide coverage so the teachers can meet with the teams they serve.

If the special needs teacher is split between multiple teams, the teams and the special needs teacher may lose the opportunity to flex the instructional time. Since these special needs teachers will have periods dedicated to serve students from more than one team, all of the teams are locked into the shared special needs teachers' schedules. This can create frustration when trying to be creative with the schedule for instruction, assessment, and team events. When the special needs teacher is attached to only one team, the teacher shares the common planning with the team and is a part of any discussion when deciding to flex the instructional time. In fact, it will often be the suggestion of the special needs teacher that will create the opportunity to flex the schedule. Teams with a special needs teacher attached will actually have many more options for authentic and common assessments, coteaching, flexible grouping of the students, and flexing instructional time.

Finally, another huge advantage of having a special needs teacher on the team is that IEPs are not only easier to schedule and manage, they are also much more meaningful. Teams should set aside a period or two (five or ten minutes) of team meeting time each week for "pre-IEPs." Teams should review the IEPs for each of the special needs students at least twice during the year prior to any IEP meetings at the end of the year. Teams should set aside five to ten minutes per student at least once each semester, preferably twice, to review the goals and progress for each special needs student.

When teams spend a little time regularly reviewing the goals and success of each special needs student, the suggestions they make for the IEPs are practical, and formulated before the formal IEP meetings. While not all of the regular education teachers on a team attend IEP meetings, they will be up-to-date with what is going on with each special needs student because of the team discussions.

Unfortunately, in other systems it is not at all unusual that the first time the regular education teacher has actually reviewed the goals and discussed the special needs student with everyone else is during the IEP meeting. In the inclusion team setting, regular education teachers have been involved in at least two, and probably four, formal discussions regarding the goals and progress of each of the special needs students before the IEP meeting. One of the benefits of inclusion is that regular education teachers are much more comfortable and confident in the IEP meeting.

Why Choose Inclusion for Instruction?

Coteaching in an inclusion classroom offers many instructional options for both the special needs and regular education teachers. All students win in an inclusion classroom. One of the most obvious advantages is better classroom management. With two teachers sharing in the instruction, there are two sets of eyes and two people to physically move around the classroom. Disciplinary situations are much less likely to happen in the first place, and intervention can be immediate should something happen. Doubling the teacher presence means more time for instruction.

The Good News About Inclusion

- Better Assessment and Feedback
- Better Classroom Management
- More Teaching Strategies for Differentiated Instruction
- More Supervision for Group and Other Special Activities
- More Individual Time for Students with a Teacher
- Shared Planning for Instruction
- More Modifications in Instruction for All Students

So, All Students Win!

Another advantage is that when two teachers share in the delivery of instruction, students are automatically exposed to different teaching styles. Two teachers are better able to plan for variety in instruction which means they teach to more learning styles. Differentiated instruction is almost automatic with two teachers planning the experiences for the students, especially when one has specialized training in creating modifications to the learning environment. When two teachers develop ideas for instruction and assessment they are going to meet the needs of more learners.

This also means that more modifications can be made for every student. There can be enrichment opportunities for the gifted and talented students, as well as more time for reteaching some students. Students receive opportunities for individualized support when there are two teachers in the classroom.

Planning for, setting up, and implementing such activities as group work, authentic assessments, labs, learning centers, and other experiential hands-on activities becomes more manageable with inclusion. Each teacher can take different aspects of each activity and the outcome is a more meaningful experience for students. Many options become possible in a two-teacher classroom that simply are impossible with only one teacher doing preparation and monitoring.

Teachers need to continually assess students to determine the need for remediation and enrichment. Authentic and formative assessments to evaluate work and determine student performances are also easier to do with two teachers. The number of opportunities to provide feedback for students grows substantially with two teachers. Adaptations and modifications for assessments, and the subsequent follow-up instruction for enrichment or remediation can also happen more regularly in the inclusion classroom.

Informal assessments to determine learning styles of the students, and customize instruction, remediation, and enrichment is better with two sets of eyes. This is especially true, once again, when one of the teachers is trained for designing custom assignments and assessments. So, regular education students as well as special needs students benefit greatly from cotaught inclusion classes. *(You know what I believe: All students win with inclusion!)*

Inclusion—The Bad News

Of course, any time there is good news, there is also bad news. One reason inclusion may not be successful is that little time is set aside for coteachers to coplan. Inadequate planning time is one of the biggest problems coteaching teams face. They must have time to prepare together to actually share in the teaching responsibilities.

Another problem that coteaching teams face is that there is often very little training in working in a two-teacher classroom. In-service can be very important to the success of coteaching. Without training, it is a shot in the dark as to whether the coteaching team will be successful or not.

It is not unlike getting your first college roommate. In a short time you either are getting along really well, or not at all, and there is often no middle ground.

No sports team would be expected to excel without training and practice. The more training and planning time coteachers have, the greater their performance will be.

The last area of concern would be the lack of personal and or professional commitment to teaching in an inclusion setting.

Despite all of the good news about inclusion, there are regular education teachers that do not believe that special needs students should be in the regular education classes. They mistakenly think that they must have lower expectations and "dummy down" their classes to meet the needs of the special needs students, if they are included in their classes. The truth, of course, is that expectations are higher across the board in inclusion classes.

There are also those special needs teachers that feel much more comfortable having their special needs students in pullout settings. They feel like they are going to have more control over the learning experience for their special needs students in a pullout setting. Without training, it can feel somewhat intimidating for the special needs teacher to go into the regular education teacher's classroom. They often feel they are invading a regular education teacher's space.

Overcoming the Obstacles

Possible Inclusion Concerns to Address

- Inadequate Planning Time
  - o The team must preschedule planning for discussion of special needs students.
  - o Time for planning for instruction and assessment with the special needs teacher
  - o The school provides some release time for planning for instruction and assessment for the inclusion teachers.
- Inadequate In-service Opportunities for Inclusion
  - o The team should make discussing and developing inclusion a part of their professional development team meeting time.
- Lack of Personal or Professional Commitment

There are several ways coplanning time might be provided for the teachers involved. The easiest way is to have the coteaching teams share the same planning period. The teachers on the team set aside some time for inclusion planning and discussing mainstreamed settings weekly. During this time, the team will plan with the special needs teacher for upcoming instruction and assessments. Remember, the team will also need to set aside time for discussing all of the special needs students to review their progress, and their needs for accommodations. "Pre IEPs" will keep everyone on the same page regarding each of the special needs students on the team.

Another way to provide some planning time outside of team meeting time is to hire a substitute teacher for either the regular education or the special education teacher. One teacher can use the substitute for a period to be off and meet with the other teacher. By rotating the substitute teacher, several coteaching teams might be able to get a period or two to plan together. Some schools use two substitute teachers, one for the regular education teachers and one for the special education teachers. In a half-day session, teachers may be able to plan for several weeks or even a month in advance. This is a very cost-effective way for school districts to provide planning time for inclusion teachers.

Some schools dedicate staff meeting time to team meetings or planning time for coteaching teams. Some schools have monthly and occasionally even weekly early-release days, or delayed-start days to provide additional team and coteaching planning time. It is important to remember that without some planning time it is easy for coteaching to become one teacher with a helper. *(However it is accomplished, planning time is critical to coteaching actually being what the name implies.)*

For the periods of time that coteaching occurs, the shared room must be "our room," and not one teacher's room that the other teacher is visiting. An in-service for coteaching can facilitate a discussion to address concerns before teachers move in together.

With training, the teachers can develop a common vision for how to develop and deliver instruction and assessments to all of the students in the classroom. There will be no YOURS or MINE, but only OURS regarding all of the students in the classroom.

Moving In Together

The team and the inclusion teachers need to decide:

- How do we share the rooms?
- Where do we put our stuff?
- How are we going to grade our students?
- How are we going to handle discipline?
- How do we introduce ourselves to the students and the parents?
- When are we going to plan?

The staff needs to be exposed to all the information possible about what inclusion and coteaching really is, and, of course, what it is not. Information and training will help alleviate anxiety and build confidence for both the regular education and the special needs teachers that will be participating in inclusion (coteaching) settings.

Scheduling Options for the Team

With the special needs teacher as part of the team, teachers can truly work as a team to determine the best placements for all of the students. The team should work with the special needs teacher to determine the best placement for all of the students within the available classes. Let's suppose the teachers on the team teach in a seven period day with an individual and team-planning period, and look at the placement options for the special needs teacher and students. This means that each of the teachers will teach five periods each day. The team has five periods to work in different combinations with the special needs teacher. Here are some scheduling options:

Pullout Programs

The options for scheduling special needs students start with pulling out those students to be with the special needs teacher for a portion of the day. For each of the five periods, the special needs teacher would pull out some of the students from the regular education classes to work in a separate room (hopefully, in the team area). Unfortunately, most pullout groups meet in a different part of the building. In this situation, the special needs teacher and the team will decide which students might benefit the most from being pulled out of the regular classroom.

Total Inclusion

At the other end of the spectrum would be all inclusion. The special needs students would be in classes with regular education students all the time. The special needs teacher would be in the room coteaching with the regular education teachers. The special needs teacher would work with the team to decide which of the five classes during the day she would be coteaching. Most often the focus is on math and language arts, but it really depends on the teachers and the IEPs. Some of the special needs students might be placed in regular education classes with modifications and consultative support from the special needs teacher. There might be paraprofessional support, but no direct instruction by the special needs teacher in the classroom.

Mainstreaming

Another option is mainstreaming, the special needs students are identified, but placed in regular education classes without additional support.

Imagine that the inclusion team has five periods, five regular education teachers, and one special needs teacher. The special needs teacher and the regular education teachers should work together with the IEPs and other student needs to determine which of the scheduling options will best meet the needs of the students on the team. The team will determine how many of the special needs students as well as any others will need each of the options. For example, the special needs teacher may end up with three or four periods of inclusion and one or two sections of pullout teaching, depending on the needs of the students in a particular year.

Pullout Programs with Regular Ed Students

If there are pullout sections, they may include some of the regular education students. Since the special needs teacher is a member of the team, the pullout class does not seem so much like a pullout class and does not have the same connotations as a traditional pullout class. It becomes just one of the team's periods of math or language arts. The special needs teacher may coteach with the math teacher for two periods and with the language arts teacher for two periods and have one period of pullout students.

It is important to be flexible enough to change the number of sections, depending on the changing needs of the students from year to year, or even within a given year. When the special needs teachers become members of teams, this is more realistic. Also, consultative support is available every day during team time regardless of the instructional situation, so that everyone is "rowing in the same direction." It is important to emphasize again that since the special needs teacher is at every team meeting, the consultative support is there for regular education students as well as the special needs students.

Additional Flexing Opportunities

With the special needs teacher on the team, additional flexible scheduling options become available. Others I have already shared become easier to implement. For example, the team can have one more assessment option for team tests when using authentic assessment. Not only can the team put in another assessment option, but this will also impact class size. An additional teacher reduces class size during assessments. The five-person team that has 125 students and averages 25 students per class can now average 21 for the assessment period.

The special needs teacher may be put into the rotation for a period of time to do a reading skills class, a study skills class, or a test-taking strategies class preceding the state standards tests. An additional person on the team gives the team one more option for working with students.

Focus on Coteaching

Coteaching is defined as two teachers in the classroom at the same time delivering instruction to all of the students. Students must see the two teachers as equals, sharing in the teaching responsibilities in the classroom. When inclusion is done correctly, the situation is not one teacher and one "helper." There can be no "your students" and "my students."

For coteaching to be successful, the two teachers must spend time planning together to design lessons and decide on the instructional responsibilities for the unit they are going to teach. There are several possible roles for each teacher to assume. The roles should be shared so that students do not see one of the teachers as always responsible for one of the roles. If the students consistently see only one of the teachers up front, they will quickly identify one of the teachers as the primary teacher, and the other as the helper.

Different roles can include delivering direct instruction, leading assessment options, providing reinforcing or enrichment instruction, and leading learning activities for applying skills being taught. In a true inclusion setting, both teachers will assume all three roles intermittently, equally, and even sometimes simultaneously.

Some Additional Notes on Planning for Inclusion: A Good Game Plan Makes all the Difference.

Successful coteaching depends on coplanning for instruction. One teacher should not do all the planning and just assign the other teacher duties during the lesson. The two teachers should be partners in the planning to ensure an equal understanding of the topic and the responsibilities each teacher will have during the instructional time. One teacher should not always be the one asking "What do you want me to do now?"

I realize that planning time may be at a premium, so teachers need to make the most of the limited amount of planning time teams might have for inclusion. That means having an efficient and effective planning process and a planning tool to make the process as easy as possible.

When the inclusion planning time is limited, teachers identify only lesson objectives and each teacher's roles and responsibilities. Teachers do not have to know exactly what the lesson will look like, but rather what the roles are going to be during the various parts of the lesson.

Follow this efficient, step-by-step plan to make the best use of planning time.

List the objectives for the lesson or series of lessons. Identify what the students will be able to do as a result of the instruction.

Develop a timeline for the lessons. How many teaching periods will be used for the instruction?

Break the lesson into three parts: the introduction (explanation), the application, and the closure (synthesis). Think about how to actively engage students in each part of the lesson. Assessment should be a continual process throughout the lesson.

Indicate what the students are going to be doing in each part of the lesson and how they are going to be assessed.

Note how the lesson will interest and motivate students by demonstrating what learning modalities and multiple intelligences will be used.

One of the goals of coteachers should be to differentiate instruction by designing lessons to meet the needs of various learners. No one lesson can include all of the multiple intelligences and learning modalities. Therefore, another goal should be to tally the types of strategies used over a period of time to learn about instructional tendencies. With two teachers sharing the planning, it is easier to develop a diversity of activities within each lesson. It is also easier to spot tendencies that can help out in future planning.

Possible Roles for Coteachers

Consider these roles as a starting point when thinking about the responsibilities each coteacher will assume.

* **Delivering direct instruction**

  The teacher takes primary responsibility for delivering instruction. As one teacher is providing the direct instruction, the other teacher may be roaming and providing individual help and providing proximity while watching for disciplinary issues

* **Leading assessment options**

  The teacher develops formative assessments and provides corrective feedback for students. The teachers can take turns reviewing work that has been reassigned to be corrected lessening the burden of evaluating student work. This can also mean designing authentic assessment options for a unit of instruction.

Multiple assessment options for a unit of instruction will require multiple rubrics for evaluating the work, and ultimately evaluating and providing feedback multiple ways, multiple times. This can be a prohibitive amount of work for one teacher.

* **Providing reinforcing or enrichment instruction**

  The teacher works with individual students as needed, or takes small groups for differentiated instruction while the other teacher provides the direct instruction to the larger group. The two teachers may split the class roughly in half, and each provides instruction simultaneously.

*** Leading learning activities for applying skills**

The teacher takes responsibility for the sections of the lesson that are designed to get the students actively involved in what's being taught. These activities may be a part of the explanation to demonstrate the concept. They might be part of the application of the lesson segment, enhancing student understanding through designing activities that require the students to use the skills they are studying. Finally, the activities may be developed to provide closure and confirm understanding of the skills that have been taught.

When coteachers use a lesson planning form, they can easily indicate how the students are going to be actively involved in each part of the lesson, and how the teachers are going to share the responsibilities. They can also indicate how they will assess each part of the lesson. Finally, teachers can indicate the Learning Styles (LS), Learning Modalities (MOD), and Multiple Intelligences (MI) that are the focus of different parts of the lesson.

Teachers may keep a calendar and weekly tallies of the various strategies they have used to motivate and reach the variety of students in their classrooms. This will validate the arsenal of strategies the teachers are already comfortable with, and the strengths the teachers already have. Teachers will continue to use these strategies, and occasionally try a new strategy from their teaching toolbox.

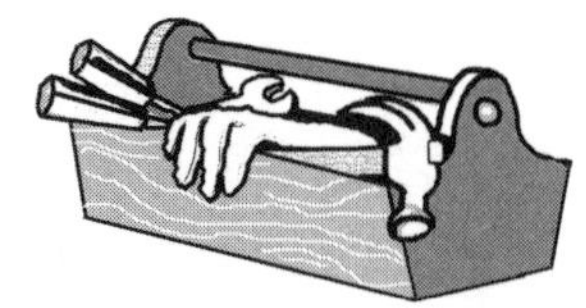

> *"If the only tool you have is a hammer, then everything looks like a nail."*
> *– Mark Twain*

Whether coteaching teams follow this procedure or one of their own, it is imperative that they have a way to plan lessons together and keep the planning process as simple as possible. If the teachers who are coteaching have limited time to plan, then a planning form will be beneficial in making the most of their planning time. (See sample form on page 176.)

COTEACHING LESSON PLANNING FORM

Teachers ______________________________ Dates ______________

Lesson Objective(s):

1. ______________________________
2. ______________________________
3. ______________________________

Explanation

Student Activity	Assessment	Accommodations LS/MOD/MI	Teacher Roles and Responsibilities

Application

Student Activity	Assessment	Accommodations LS/MOD/MI	Teacher Roles and Responsibilities

Closure/Processing

Student Activity	Assessment	Accommodations LS/MOD/MI	Teacher Roles and Responsibilities

TAG . . . You're It!

Coteaching

Exercises one and two are for any regular education and special needs teachers that may be coteaching. In exercise three, teachers get on teams to practice pre-IEPs. A little time spent upfront helps teams and special needs teachers save hours when it comes time for writing the actual IEPs.

Exercise One: Getting the Team Ready to Play.

Teachers discuss various issues that they will face together as they coteach. Imagine that you and a partner are going to give a workshop on each of the topics listed. Both of you are strong teachers and either could do any of the workshops. However, this is a time to look carefully at your training and the materials you have on hand that would make it easier to do the workshop.

So during the discussion, share the materials and training you have, and then decide which of you will be presenting each workshop. Each teacher should present an equal number of workshops, so negotiate and trade workshops until each of you has the same number. Then write your initials beside the workshops you will be doing.

Which workshops would you do?

Special Educator	Workshop Topics	Regular Educator
________	Classroom Management	________
________	Assessment of State Standards	________
________	Authentic Assessment	________
________	Parent Involvement	________
________	Learning Styles	________
________	Differentiated Instruction	________
________	Content Knowledge	________
________	Organizational Skills	________
________	Large Group Instruction	________
________	Instructional Modifications	________
________	Student Motivation	________
________	Curriculum Alignment with State Standards	________

Processing the Activity

The purpose of this activity is to take time to share your experiences, training, and materials regarding each topic. After this discussion, you will have a base of knowledge about the previous experiences you each have had and some of the things you each bring to planning and coteaching a lesson.

Of course, each item on the list leads to other discussions, and you should feel free to add to the list as you go. When you discuss classroom management, you will become familiar with each other's discipline philosophies and decide how you will handle different classroom management issues. You still have to learn by doing, but you will have some sense of how you will begin to deal with your students. When you discuss modifications and classroom adjustments, you will also discuss grading. When you discuss organizational skills, you will need to decide how you are going to physically organize to room. Preplanning and discussion lead to confidence and much less anxiety.

I had put together a bulletin board decorated with various Space Shuttle pictures and NASA information. I have to admit that I had not changed that bulletin board for quite some time, but I also liked it very much. When I first cotaught with a special needs teacher, she suggested that we might want to change that bulletin board, and needless to say I did not want to do that at all. She came up with a compromise, saying that I could keep the bulletin board for three months, after which I would allow her to change it. Reluctantly I agreed.

The very next day I came into the classroom, and she had already changed the bulletin board! I had to admit that she was very creative and that her bulletin board actually looked much better than mine, but I was upset because we had made a deal. So I asked her what had happened to the three months that I was supposed to get, to which she smiled and replied, "I forgot to mention that the three months you get are June, July, and August!"

We actually got along quite well and were very successful coteachers; however, we did not have any training at the time. That meant that we had to figure things out as we went. We were lucky, but with training and preliminary planning, every coteaching team can be successful without having to count on luck.

Exercise Two: Putting the Game Plan Together!

Plan a lesson. Get with your coteaching partner and fill out a Coteaching Lesson Planning Form. Copy the one on page 176 or create one of your own.

Remember that each teacher should have about the same amount of responsibility for the lesson. Decide what roles and responsibilities you each will take for each of the three parts of the lesson. The explanation, application, and synthesis parts of the lesson each have a student activity, accommodations, and assessment, so there are at least six opportunities to share the roles and responsibilities for the lesson.

Discuss each part of the lesson. You will begin to understand your partner. Just as importantly, you will have the opportunity to learn from each other and grow professionally. The first few lessons may take a little more time, but as the teachers work together, this time will decrease dramatically.

Exercise Three: Teaming Up for Special Needs Students—Doing IEP Warm-ups!

Set aside 15 minutes of team meeting time to meet with the special needs teacher assigned to your team. The team and the special needs teacher will review three IEPs of special needs students on your team. Have a timer ready; establish five minutes as the amount of time for the discussion of each of the students.

First, make sure each teacher understands the parameters of an IEP. Briefly review the current placement and assess the student's success. Are immediate interventions needed? Look at long-term issues that might be addressed at the next IEP or review meeting.

Select three special needs students to discuss. Use the timer to indicate five minutes for the discussion of each student. If you have students from multiple special needs teachers attached to your team, select students from only one of the special needs teacher's case loads for your discussion. The special needs teacher should be in attendance.

The special needs teacher gives a synopsis of the IEP. Regular education teachers review the current placements along with the successes and challenges in relation to the goals of the current IEP. Consider what changes, if any, the team might suggest. Depending on caseload and team size, each special needs student should be discussed minimally twice a year, and possibly even once a marking period in a pre-IEP meeting.

The Four Stages of Coteaching and Interdisciplinary Team Development

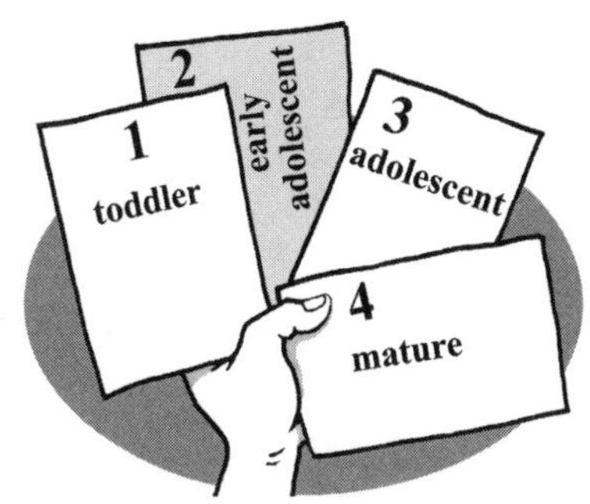

Whenever two or more teachers are put into a situation where they have to work together for an extended period of time, they go through four phases of development. All interdisciplinary teams, coteaching teams, and other groups such as school improvement committees will go through these four phases on their way to becoming high-performing teams. I like to look at the stages of change in terms of human development and use the acronym TEAM (**T**oddler, **E**arly Adolescent, **A**dolescent, **M**ature).

It is important for all involved to understand the stages of team development and to recognize where their team is on the continuum. All teams will progress through these phases at different rates. While some teams move through the phases more quickly or slowly, the speed is not an indicator of the team's long-term success. With proper coaching and teacher commitment, all teams can become high-performing teams.

Each time I reference coteaching teams specifically, the descriptors also apply to interdisciplinary teams. When interdisciplinary teams add new members, they go through the same stages with the new member.

Stage One: Toddler

The first phase of team development is the toddler phase. During the toddler phase, teachers build their initial levels of trust and spend lots of time dealing with process. Teachers are just getting to know about each other's grading policies and discipline styles. They are busy figuring out how they will organize their space. It is important to establish priorities and settle on the guiding principles for their cotaught class.

In-service is critical prior to, and during, the toddler phase of team development. The focus during this phase is on the mechanical. Teachers are learning about their roles and responsibilities. That means they are in the early stages of deciding what they are going to do and how they are going to do it. They will still be very independent and will look at each part of a lesson as "your part" or "my part." They do not know each other well enough to answer for each other and will most often defer questions between each other.

During stage one both teachers on a coteaching team will decide on the roles during lessons, but will still do much of their planning individually. They know they will be working together, but will still look at how things will impact them individually during training.

As teachers work through the toddler phase, they will focus on tasks. While they accomplish the various tasks and learn how to work together, they begin to build the level of trust that will be critical to the success of the coteaching team. When some of the mechanics are practiced and a level of trust is achieved, the coteaching team will be ready to take on higher levels of shared instruction.

Notes on Coteaching — Stage One

- **Early Childhood**
  The teachers are just beginning to find the team's balance.
- **Building Trust**
  Partners work through issues to build trust.
  Trust-building activities can help.
- **Establishing Purpose and Guiding Principles**
  Partners have to develop a common vision of teaching early adolescents.
- **In-Service Is Critical**
  Training increases performance and helps limit anxiety.
  In-service should include all teaming topics. The topics will seem more relevant since the teachers are now doing what they only studied and discussed before.
- **Need for Information**
  Feedback is very important.
  Communication skills are developing. These skills will determine the pair's quality of information exchange.
  Quality and quantity of information can help address confusion.
- **Establish Teaching Parameters and Set Policies**
  For coteaching teams, the teachers have to decide on classroom layout, lesson design, homework, discipline, and bulletin boards.
  For interdisciplinary teams, the teachers have to decide on common discipline policies. (See the Team Management Chapter.)
- **Individual Learning**
  The teachers tend to learn in reference to their personal situation.
- **Feelings**
  Teachers experience excitement, anxiety, confusion.

Stage Two: Early Adolescent

As with human development, this is the hormonal period of development. It is the time feelings become an integral part of the coteaching team process. During this stage personalities come "front and center" in the working relationship. *(Without a doubt, this is the most difficult part of the team-building process.)*

It is during this stage of development that teachers need to apply their problem-solving and communication skills. Therefore, it is imperative that conflict resolution be a part of the training for coteaching teams. The teams need to be able to assess their performance and identify areas in need of improvement. Hopefully, they have been trained to look at issues and not personalities. It is in this stage that teams without adequate training hit the wall.

As teams work through stage two they begin to see they can handle anything as long as they support each other. Teams open to self-assessment and those willing to make adaptations are the most successful. As coteaching teams move through stage two, they master the art of compromise, which develops a strong connection between the teachers. While there may be feelings of stress and frustration during this stage, teachers also get a great feeling of accomplishment as they become a stronger team.

Notes on Coteaching — Stage Two

- **Puberty**
  (Need I say more?)
- **Most Difficult Time**
  If a team is going to have a rough spot, this is it.
- **Deal with Personalities**
  Teachers have to move past the mechanics to acknowledge and accommodate each team member's individual style and personality.
  Competition can occur between team members.
- **Master the Mechanics**
  Processes like "Thumbs Up" and "COW" meetings are taking shape.
- **In-Service Should Include:**
  (Teachers share more, but still learn independently.)
  team meeting management;
  curriculum development;
  beginning discussions of learning connections;
  continued effective communication, trust and consensus building, and problem solving;
  student management.
- **Feelings**
  Teachers experience ccomplishment, connectedness, stress, frustration.

Stage Three: Adolescent

Adolescence is still a time of great change, and many challenges still lie ahead. However, the adolescent team member has a clear vision of what inclusion should be and has developed habits, work skills, and intrinsic motivation to move through the stage. There is still much to learn, but teachers know what to look for and therefore they will be much more targeted in their search for information.

In stages one and two, teachers learned some things from their colleagues but were still focused on themselves. It is in stage three that coteachers become very open to learning from their coteaching partner. They now have well-developed intuition about how their partners think and how they will probably respond in a given situation. Teachers in stage three have found common ground for discipline and other student management issues. The teachers empower each other and feel much more comfortable speaking for each other which they begin to do with great confidence.

Stage three is exciting and motivating for the teachers because they do not have to worry about hurting each other's feelings, and they can focus on the fun stuff! This is when the teachers really start to share instructional strategies and actually codevelop strategies for each lesson. They are accustomed to making adaptations and can begin to get creative with assessments as well as instruction. To the students, the teachers have been coteaching all along; but to the teachers, this is when they really feel like they are sharing totally in the instruction, discipline, and assessment. It is during this stage that teachers feel like they are truly coteaching.

Notes on Coteaching — Stage Three

- **High Levels of Collaboration**
  Team members have worked through power issues.
  Roles and responsibilities for the team are freely shared among the team members.
  Teachers have discussed and developed multiple learning connections.
- **Consensus Is More Easily Achieved**
  Team members have learned about each other's priorities and make accommodations for each other.
- **Teachers Empower Each Other.**
  Team members have learned how to agree to disagree, move on, and still back each other up.
  Team members are open to "Thumbs Up" and COW suggestions.
- **Group Learning**
  Team members are beginning to see training through the eyes of the group as well as individually.

- **In-Service Should Include:**
  Student learning;instructional strategies; authentic assessment; curriculum integration.
- **Little or No Competition**
  Teachers have learned that success for any team member is success for the entire team.
- **Common Voice**
  Team members are consistent with their policies.
  A common language has been developed for student referrals, COWs, and other team procedures.
- **Feelings**
  Teachers experience control, support, empowerment, confidence.

Stage Four: Mature

Coteaching teams have reached stage four when they finish sentences for each other. There are not the pauses that may have happened in previous stages while the teachers were figuring out what they were going to do. They move between roles and responsibilities smoothly and communicate effectively nonverbally. A nod or a gesture with the eyes says as much now as a conversation would have in previous stages. Simply put, the teachers have developed a very high level of communication. The mature team has developed complete trust and the knowledge that each teacher has the support of the other.

With the high level of collaboration that comes in stage four, the mature team is free to try things they might not have thought about before. They will integrate their class with other classes, and share skills and assessments. They will be ready to look at yearlong projects and interdisciplinary units that weave skills from other areas.

When a mature team attends an in-service training, they learn together. Before this stage each teacher would attend an in-service training, and individuals would listen and gather information. Now it also natural for them to process information in terms of how their partners would be impacted and what the pair would do with it together.

Coteaching has often been compared to a marriage. In the beginning of a marriage you are just trying to figure out who is going to be doing what. You have to decide who gets what part of the closet and where you will each put your items in the house. Then "the honeymoon is over." The marriage has entered stage two. Your partner's habits that seemed so cute become annoying, and you have to work through those issues. Marriages in stage three know what it takes, and have learned enough to be successful if they are willing to make the efforts required. In stage four, the couple thinks alike, and one can anticipate the other's reactions in almost any situation.

Notes on Coteaching — Stage Four

- **Adult Stage**
  Team members feel more in control.
  The team members now feel like teaming is working for them, instead of them working for the team.
- **Teachers Are in Alignment with Each Other**
  A high level of trust has been established.
  A common language has emerged.
  The mechanics of teaming are second nature.
  Teachers begin to anticipate each other and often finish sentences for each other.
- **Consensus Is Easily Achieved**
  Team members have learned about each other's priorities and make accommodations for each other.
  The team handles politics in a straightforward manner.
- **In-Service Should Include:**
  Differentiated instruction; process of learning; and project-based learning, using curriculum integration, learning connections, and shared assessments.
- **All Team Members Share Roles and Responsibilities Freely**
- **Group Learning**
  Team members see training through the eyes of the group, as well as individually.
  The team, as a team, embraces professional development.
- **Team Members Take Responsibility for Each Other**
  Team members are confident in representing, and being represented by, each other.
- **Feelings**
  Teachers experience collaboration, freedom, control, confidence.

TAG . . . You're It!

Coteaching

Exercise One

Discuss the four stages of team development. Use the descriptors of each stage of team development to decide what stage of development you are in currently. Depending on the stage of development your team is in, the discussion should then focus on how to move to the next level.

Exercise Two

Develop a plan for coteaching two lessons. Decide who will be responsible for each portion of the lesson. Be careful to balance who is leading the direct instruction so that both teachers share equal "authority."

Team-based Advisory Programs

Building a Strong Heart For Your Team and School

Getting Started

The heart is the largest muscle in the body, and whether a person is trying to get into shape or maintain their level of fitness, cardiovascular endurance plays an integral role. If the heart is not working well, the rest of the muscles cannot be developed. In addition, the heart connects the rest of the body as it sends blood on its continual circular trip. Every organ depends on the heart.

Like the heart, the advisory program runs through the entire school, and is usually the only class that all teachers have in common. The skills that are taught in advisory are essential for the school to develop to its fullest potential. Advisory programs should be team based and focused on building skills. *(The school should diagnose student needs and identify the skills that should be taught as a part of the advisory program.)*

Advisory programs should target skills that students need. In this chapter, these skills will be called "student skills."

These "student skills" include affective skills, the skills that make for successful students beyond the cognitive reading or math levels. In education, teachers tend to teach the student affective skills by consequence, rather than by direct instruction. A teacher may explain to a student that she is failing because she does not pay attention well, or she is disorganized, or she does not follow directions. The teacher assumes that the student will then make the corrections to learn how to listen, become more organized, or follow directions better.

Organizational skills and listening skills are skills that can be taught, just as correct grammar can be taught. Unfortunately, teachers already have more content in their curriculum than they can address in a school year. Therefore, they often do not take time out of their curriculum to teach lessons on listening skills, organizational skills, and how to follow directions well. High-performing schools that choose to address the affective skill issue will usually shorten each period and use the minutes gained to create a new period for advisory programs.

To emphasize the importance of affective skills, just go to any major bookstore and look in the business section; check out how many books there are to teach these skills. Businesses spend big money to reinforce and teach their workers, and especially their executives, affective skills.

The good news is that an effective advisory program can have a huge impact on the success of teachers, teams, and the entire school. Advisory can be a powerful tool for teams to use to achieve cognitive, as well as affective goals. An effective advisory program will help insure success for all students by enhancing and setting the tone for the academic portion of the day. By developing the specific affective skills required for cognitive success, advisory will create a positive and challenging learning environment.

The bad news is that selling and developing ownership in an advisory program can be very difficult. Even maintaining advisory programs in schools that already have programs can be a challenge.

I often hear teachers talking about not being counselors, and not wanting to do any of that "touchy-feely, froufrou" stuff! It is critical that teachers understand they DO NOT have to become counselors, and there is nothing touchy-feely or froufrou about a meaningful advisory program. To that end, it is important that teachers and all other stakeholders have a clear understanding of the purpose of advisory so that they can actively support the program. An effective advisory program can be used to address many student and team needs that cannot be addressed in other classes.

A school with a great advisory program means a school with a "lot of heart." Advisory is the place where we do exercises to build and maintain a strong heart. Advisory is our cardiovascular workout each day. We work to build skills, willingness, endurance, and motivation to go the distance! To this end, the goal of an effective advisory program is to target and build specific affective skills necessary for long-term student success. Later in this chapter, you will participate in an exercise to identify the specific skills your school needs to develop as a part of your advisory program.

What's in a Name?

If the staff, students, parents, and the community understand the purpose of advisory, they will also understand how important the advisory program is. Therefore, you will want to give your advisory program a name. Giving your advisory program a name will reflect the importance of the program. *(Some of the names I have seen include: Impact, Viking Time, Challenge, Prime Time, and PRIDE.)* Giving advisory a name puts it up there with algebra, American government, literature, and physical science.

Another way to demonstrate the importance of advisory is to make a students' advisor the first point of contact for parents, and for any questions they may have about their student. As teachers work with students in advisory, they will generally be best able to answer any generic questions parents may have about their student's involvement. Also, in schools with portfolio assessments, the student portfolios are often kept in the advisory room, and the advisor helps the students with their portfolio management.

Whenever possible, an advisory program is a wonderful way to start the school day. If you fish, you will understand why I sometimes reference advisory as the time for the teachers to "set the hook." When fishing, you work the lure to get the fish really excited to the point of taking the bait. At that point you want to set the hook. Of course, some fish escape, and we do not get them into the boat; but we cannot even try to get them in the boat until we have a good hook set.

It is the same with students. Every morning we want to get students ready and excited about learning; we want to get them "hooked" for the day. Then the rest of the day we are just trying to reel in the catch. Teachers need to look at every day as another opportunity to "set the hook."

Using Advisory to Get the "Heart" of the School in Shape

One of the primary goals of teaming is to create "small communities for learning." There are many benefits to living in a small community. In small communities, everyone knows everyone else, community members support each other, people feel safer, and take great pride in being a part of a small community. Advisory is a tool to help us build the foundation for our small communities for learning. With a team-based advisory, we can use the program to develop a strong team identity, work on student skills, and build a challenging, yet safe, learning environment.

Advisory is also the tool that will help teachers fill in all the blanks, and do things that do not fit in a specific content area. For example, some schools use advisory to teach students about how they learn. Students may do activities to learn about how their brain works and study multiple intelligences. Then the students will learn how to apply the brain-based training in their different classroom settings.

Advisory is a great place to do team-building activities, and academic preparation activities to teach things like organizational skills, how to follow directions, and review study techniques. Teams can also run their Thumbs Up program, and provide follow-up support through advisory. The idea is that advisory helps students see at least one teacher as their advocate. (See a list of resources dealing with advisory in the Appendix.)

In keeping with the small community idea, advisory should be team based, with students assigned to advisory groups by team. It is wonderful if every teacher in the building is involved with the advisory program. The administrative team in many buildings also has advisory groups. Having all of the staff involved increases ownership, and lowers class size. That way, exploratory teachers and administrators can be assigned to teams, and their advisory students come from those teams.

I need to mention that students certainly can be assigned to advisory teachers in cross-grade level groups. This organization can provide opportunities for things like mentoring, and a student can have one advisor all the way through the middle school. However, having students from multiple grade levels in one advisory group eliminates the ability to do anything in advisory that might be grade-level or team based. If the advisory program is not team based, teachers will not be able to do any academic follow-up, get ready for field trips, or tie in thematic activities. For these and other management and organizational reasons, and because keeping the small community of learning intact is important to me, I highly recommend that Advisory groups be team based if you have teams.

Preparation for Advisory

In workshops on advisory programs, I talk about taking out three Ps, and putting in one P. The three Ps that should be removed from advisory *(as much as possible)* are *paper*, *pencil*, and *preparation*. There are many great paper and pencil activities, but we do not want advisory to become another worksheet period. I also understand how much time teachers already put into planning for their other classes, so I very much want to minimize the amount of time of preparation for advisory.

Teams should meet one day a week to review and prepare for their advisory program. When the process is shared, the planning should take about 15 minutes of team time per week. To help minimize the amount of planning time, teachers take turns at planning a week of advisory lessons. That way, if there are six teachers doing advisory for a team, each teacher only needs to plan once every six weeks. Each teacher develops lessons for advisory six times a year. *(By the way, reviewing and planning for advisory is a great way to start team meetings on Fridays.)*

Each week the team should review how advisory went that week. "Smart" teams will keep an advisory binder, inserting the activities they liked each week into the binder. Eventually the team will have a binder full of successful activities. Keeping the activities in a binder with the dates will help prevent the team from continually "reinventing the wheel."

The other thing that happens each week when the team discusses advisory is that the teacher responsible shares the schedule and activities for the upcoming week. The teacher lists any needed materials, and answers any questions about the activities.

With experience, a team will also start to organize the binder, moving certain activities to more appropriate times of the year. Some activities, such as "The Ultimate Test Review" from the book Fire Up for Learning, will be used several times a year, as teams learn to give common tests. The teachers will also develop advisory activities that will work well with interdisciplinary units and projects that they develop over time. As the advisory binder grows, planning for advisory becomes even easier.

As with all things we do in life, we get better with practice, and advisory is no different. The planning and use of the advisory time becomes second nature when teams have been together for a while, and have accumulated resources and materials to handle a variety of issues. Effective teams will use advisory to enhance what they have happening on the team. For example, the team may be experiencing multicultural issues and will want to do some multicultural activities to discuss and teach tolerance with the students. So the team will adjust what they were going to be doing in advisory to include the activities. Advisory should be flexible, and the curriculum should never be set or "locked in." Teachers should have access to numerous resources and materials, as well as the flexibility to use them as needs demand.

Advisory is a time to work with students on setting goals, and is a great time to review and assess goals as students go through the year. Advisory can be used to review each student's progress, recognize student efforts individually, and to get students ready for upcoming events like tests. However, advisory is **never** a study hall. It is important that all of the students are actively engaged during advisory.

- Before the first science labs or math learning center activities, why not use advisory to build the groups and teach the students how to work together within a group setting?
- If a series of conflict issues develop, advisory would be a great place to do some conflict resolution and peer-mentoring activities.
- If there is a team test coming up, the Ultimate Test Review activity is a great way to get students actively engaged, working together, and improving performance on the test.

So two important keys to the success of any advisory program are:

1) Provide an adequate amount of training for teacher advisors. Training should include demonstrating how to find, develop, and implement appropriate activities for the current targeted skills.

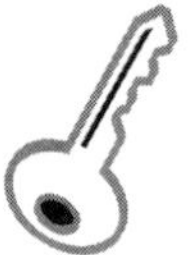

2) Provide a wealth of resources and materials to make preparation as easy as possible. Creating a library of resources for advisory is now easier than ever.

In addition, teachers and administrators must clearly define the purpose of the advisory program.

Get Your Advisory Pumping with Purpose

We want every student to identify with at least one significant adult in the building. The student should see this adult as his or her advocate. Advisory should be the safest time in a student's day, and to that end, the advisory time is not graded. This is a time to enhance the relationships between students, and between students and teachers, to create the most effective learning environment possible.

The mistake many schools make is that they just tell their teachers they have a 25- or 30-minute block called advisory. During that block teachers are directed to "build relationships with the students." (This is how advisory programs have earned the "touchy-feely, froufrou" descriptors.) All the relationships built should be skill based, with the student and teacher recognizing that they are going to work together to help maximize experiences within the learning environment. Teachers and students both must recognize that the program will be student centered and skill based. When student success is the focus, advisory programs are immensely successful.

The student-to-teacher relationship is probably the most important factor in student success. Participating in an advisory program will help both students and teachers understand each other at a higher level. This does not mean that teachers must be "friends," or most certainly, counselors for the students. Advisory is a time for students and teachers to work together to develop a better understanding of how teaching and learning works.

Each school is different, and your advisory program should be designed accordingly to meet the needs of the students in your school. Ask the basic question: "What skills do our students need to be successful in our school?" The answer to that question, along with the development and implementation of those skills should be the basis of your advisory program.

> *"I don't care what you know, until I know that you care"*
> *– Anonymous*

A bus driver in Chicago made my responsibility as a teacher and especially as an advisor clear to me. I was working with schools in the Chicago area, and had the opportunity to ride public transportation into downtown from the western suburbs. I needed to arrive just south of the Loop, so I decided to get an early start and take the bus instead of driving. I was not looking forward to the long ride to the school during morning traffic. As I got on the bus, the driver was in the middle of telling a joke. It was one that I had heard before, but this guy was telling it with such feeling that I found myself laughing as he finished.

The bus driver was an enormous man. I looked at him in the mirror, and his face filled it, not only because of his size, but also due to a huge smile. He told jokes and funny stories, one right after the other, all the way into the downtown area. I was laughing so hard that my side was hurting, and I almost missed getting off at my stop. I did not notice that I had been on this bus for nearly an hour. The driver had even made up jokes from stories in that day's newspaper! At one point he had us all laughing so hard that the man sitting next to me starting slapping my knee. I thought that the driver must work in one of the comedy clubs in the area. He definitely sounded like a professional comedian.

As I was getting off the bus, I asked him if he worked at one of Chicago's comedy clubs, hoping that I could go see him there. He shared that people asked him that same question all the time, but that he didn't work at any of the clubs. He said, "Driving this bus is my only job." I looked at him and told him what a great ride it had been and that he was very good at his job. He stopped me and said, "Isn't that what it is all about?" I asked him what he meant by this.

The bus driver said, "Mister, I bring people into downtown to work in those buildings every day. I know that they have very tough jobs, and I can usually see the stress on their faces as they get on my bus. So I figure that if they get off of my bus feeling better about going to work than they did when they got on my bus, the city of Chicago will run well today. Suppose I didn't do anything at all, or was short with my riders. Well, then the city of Chicago would not run as well today. And you know what, Mister?" (He said this with great feeling, pointing a finger for *emphasis.) "It is up to **ME** how well the city of Chicago runs." I was totally blown away by this man's personal commitment to the success of his city.*

*This driver felt that it was his **personal responsibility** to get his passengers ready for their day at work. That is what the advisory program should be all about. If we can start each day doing something to help our students be more successful and feel better about being in school, then our schools will run better. Hopefully, the teachers will take the kind of personal responsibility that the bus driver demonstrated. Every teacher needs to understand that he or she is individually responsible for how each day starts for students, and how well our schools run. One thing is certain, starting the day off with a motivating, challenging, skill-based, fun advisory program will help your school run better than ever!*

The equation for student success has multiple components. One part of the equation is the teacher. A highly-skilled teacher will create a learning environment which will actively engage students in motivating, challenging, well-designed lessons. Successful teachers will do everything they can to meet the needs of every student.

The other main part of the equation is the student. Teachers can do their best to deliver instruction in the most effective ways possible, but there are some things that students must do as well to get the most out of any lesson. Students need to feel as responsible for their learning as the teachers do. Students need to learn that education is not something that is done to them, but rather something that should be done with them. This means that students need to have the skills necessary to be more responsible for their learning, and take an active role in the learning process.

Back to the Heart of the School

When you hear someone say something like, "He has a lot of heart!" it usually means one of two things. An athlete may perform beyond all expectations and seemingly beyond even physical ability. When we hear of such athletes pulling off amazing feats, we refer to them as *having a lot of heart*. When people say you have a lot of heart, they may mean that you consistently give your best to tasks, and will do whatever it takes to get the job done. So having a lot of heart involves demonstrating focus, ownership, motivation, leadership, teamwork, and tenacity, and exerting maximum effort. These are skills that need to be developed in students if you want to have a school with strong heart.

At other times people describe someone as having a lot of heart because that person is very empathetic and cares about the needs of others. The person identifies that someone is struggling, and is able to respond appropriately to provide the support needed. These individuals know when praise is needed; they find ways to celebrate deserving efforts and accomplishments. So, having a lot of heart also means demonstrating interpersonal skills, the ability to communicate effectively, the ability to identify and solve problems, and the willingness to be a contributing part of the community. These are skills that also must be developed for a school to have a strong heart.

The overachieving athlete and the empathetic person both have a philosophy that can best be summed up in the phrase "failure is not an option."

When visiting schools, I often ask teachers why they do advisory. The most common answer may not surprise you. They do not answer me with a philosophical reason or quote research about the affective needs of early adolescents. Most often, they simply tell me they do advisory because they were told that they have to do it.

The focus of advisory programs should be student success. There are many things that factor into helping a student become more successful. Students know the consequences of not being able to focus well or listen well or follow directions well, but we often do not actually take the time to "teach" them how to do these things.

Have you ever heard teachers say that they would use cooperative learning more as an instructional strategy if their students would work better in cooperative groups? *(Perhaps the students would, if they could.)* Many students have never had "training" for working productively in groups. In fact, many teachers have not had that kind of training. *(We often misinterpret not doing certain things as a "won't," when, in fact, it is really a "can't" or a "don't know how.")*

Advisory is the perfect place to actually teach all students those skills that do not seem to fit in other areas of our curriculum. Advisory is the time we are able to work with our students in a safe, nongraded, supportive, motivating, and challenging atmosphere. Students will come to see their advisors as advocates. With teams, we build small communities for learning, and with advisory groups, we build the "homes" in our community. *(A good advisory program makes sure that each home has a porch.)*

As we become better advisors we also become better teachers in our other classes. In advisory we learn how to

- run and process activities to make them more meaningful;
- identify and develop affective skills; and
- meet the affective, as well as the cognitive needs of our early adolescents.

And we will get better results in all of our classes!

Just as the bus driver prepared his riders for their day, the teachers must get their students ready to be successful, which will in turn determine how well their school will run. A skill-based, purpose-driven advisory program can be the bus, and you can be the driver that motivates the students to do their very best in their job as students. We want to change all of the "can'ts" and "won'ts" to "cans" and "wills." With a clearly defined purpose, meaningful activities, and a dedicated staff implementing your advisory program, there is no question that your school will run well.

Advisory Activity

Skill to be Taught:

Description of the Activity:

Background Info:

Materials Needed:

TAG . . . You're It!

Get Your School Pumping with Purpose

In the following exercises, you and your team will work together to identify the skill areas needed by early adolescents to be successful in your classrooms and in your school. You will also discover how to select appropriate activities to build student skills for the areas selected for your advisory program. Finally, you will see how to process the activities to help students develop the student skills.
As you and your team work through the following activities, the purpose of your advisory program should be clarified.

Exercise One: Developing a Purpose-Driven Advisory Program

In this activity you are going to develop the purpose for your advisory program and take a closer look at the student side of the equation.

- What are some of the things students could do?
- What kinds of student skills would make you a better teacher? Consider for a moment what students need to do to ensure that they are taking full advantage of your lessons.

While no one is perfect, let's daydream for a while. Imagine that in your dream you have a classroom full of perfect students. *(Perfect students do not all make great grades, but they do make the best grade possible for them.)* Think about the kind of effort and the skills that would make for perfect students in the perfect classroom.

Your wish list might look something like this:

- Do homework
- Come prepared for class
- Participate in class discussions
- Respect others
- Listen actively
- Follow directions
- Persevere
- Work in a group successfully
- Focus on an objective
- Stay on task
- Paraphrase what is read
- Ask meaningful and appropriate questions

Now think about the school as a whole. What kinds of things do students need if they are to have a successful middle school experience? We want all students to take full advantage of all that your school has to offer. This will require a variety of efforts and skills from our students, depending on where they are in your school. What will those efforts and skills include? We often find ourselves thinking something like, *that student would be so much more successful if he or she would just* . . . . Complete that statement for the students in your building. You will have identified their needs.

List all the things students could be doing to make your classroom a better place to learn. Think about the skills students need to make the most out of their middle school experience. Consider how you would complete the following statement:

> I could teach any student anything if the student would (or could) just ________ , and ________ , and ________ .

Fill in as many of the blanks as your team can.

As you consider the statement, use a couple of your classlists. Think about the needs of each of your students individually, from the most difficult to the hardest working, as well as from the lowest level to the most gifted. Consider what students could do to help you, as the teacher, move them from wherever they are to wherever the next level might be for them. In other words, what could each student do to become more successful? This list of needs for your students will become the guide for your advisory program.

Example:

Georgia could be even more successful in my classroom if she would (or could) just:

- follow directions better
- focus (on what I need her to focus on)
- listen
- ask questions
- trust me
- not interrupt the class so often
- not give up so easily
- practice
- ask better questions
- participate
- respect herself and others
- get to school more often
- get to my class on time
- organize her thoughts better
- work with others in cooperative groups
- take better notes
- get herself organized
- gain a better understanding of how she learns
- come to my class prepared
- think before acting

Make a list of all the things you can think of that will help your students become more successful in your building. *(It might also be argued that these skills would make your students more successful in life as well.)*

Most staffs create lists with 50 to 100 items. Often each item on the list will lead to several more related items. So make your list as comprehensive as you can, and know that you, your teammates, and the school will be adding to the list over time as you identify new needs for your students. Simply put, every day in advisory should relate to something on your list.

Some schools will take the exercise one step further, and categorize the list. They will group together items that are most alike. This can be helpful because it can give them general areas with specific topics in each area. For example, if you group items from your lists, some of the groups might include similar related needs like:

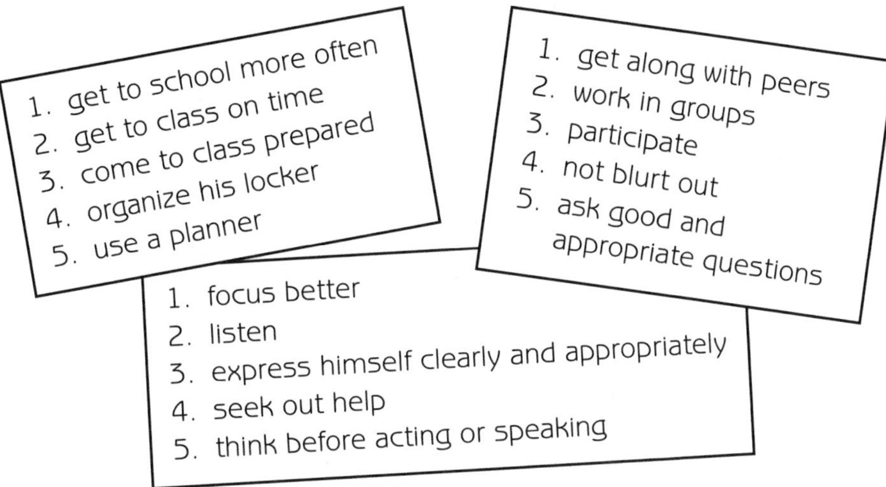

1. get to school more often
2. get to class on time
3. come to class prepared
4. organize his locker
5. use a planner
1. get along with peers
2. work in groups
3. participate
4. not blurt out
5. ask good and appropriate questions
1. focus better
2. listen
3. express himself clearly and appropriately
4. seek out help
5. think before acting or speaking

As you will quickly see, these groups represent organization, communication, and respect and responsibility. Each group overlaps other groups. There will be no clear lines delineating the groups; however, the organized groups of student needs may help you accumulate appropriate materials.

It is important to note that there will always be student needs on the list over which the teachers at the school have very little control. One of your lists should include needs similar to these:

1. get enough sleep
2. have breakfast
3. have a place to do homework at home
4. have someone to help with homework
5. have good hygiene
6. have parental support

Of course, you want to help students with these issues, so I recommend that schools share those things we have little control over with the parents. In your newsletters, remind parents periodically about the importance of such things as enough sleep, a good breakfast, and a place and a time to do homework. You can also post these items at events like open houses, concerts, and athletic competitions. Many schools have parent nights and include a topic for helping parents better understand how they can best support their student's academic efforts. I am often asked to demonstrate an advisory activity or two at parent meetings, and it is always fun to show parents what the program is all about. So your school might consider making advisory an essential part of your parent programs.

When one school did exercise one, they started out with nearly 100 individual items. When they catergorized their items, they came up with about ten different categories. Some of the categories included communication, social interaction, respect, responsibility, organization, cooperation, problem solving, and teamwork. Each item on the various lists represented a specific need in that area. Again, several items fit in more than one list, and that is fine. When you look for activities for your program, they will often be listed in categories like these. Remember that most activities fit into multiple categories, so you and your team should select the most appropriate skill area for each activity.

The important thing is that your list of student needs is based on the characteristics of the early adolescents in your particular building. The purpose of advisory is to help meet the needs for student success in your building. I recommend that the purpose of your advisory program, and the skills you develop as a part of the program, be shared with the students, parents, and school board members. It is important that all the stakeholders in the school understand why you are implementing this program called advisory.

Sample Advisory Purpose Statement

The purpose of the advisory program at Exemplary Middle School is to help our students develop the skills needed to maximize their potential for success.

(The bottom line in advisory: Every day the teachers do activities to help students develop skills identified by their school as necessary for student success. Just as in any other class, the teacher and the students should be able to indicate skills. There is absolutely no fluff in a skill-based, purpose-driven advisory program.)

Exercise Two: Selecting and Implementing Advisory Activities.

Team members should share the responsibility for selecting advisory activities. When the program gets going, each team member may take a week and prepare the advisory activities for that week.

For this activity, select a few activities that you feel address one or more of the skill areas identified by the team. Share the activities you selected. Check your lists of needs and select one or more advisory activities to use with your students.

Another bonus of sharing in the responsibility of finding activities for advisory is the establishing of norms for what is an appropriate advisory activity. As team members share the activities they think represent certain skill areas, the rest of the team evaluates how the skill areas are interpreted. Through discussion, the team achieves consensus regarding what types of activities help students develop appropriate skills.

After you and your teammates have selected activities, try some of the activities with your students. If you do not have an advisory program, you might want to try these activities at the end of your periods. Your team might also create a rotating drop schedule as described in the scheduling chapter, and do advisory activities with your students during the extra period. Be sure to relate the skills in the activity to skills on your list. So, you might say something to the students like, "Now I will be a better teacher, and you will be more successful students, if we will just *follow directions* and *work together*, as we did in this activity."

You might use a group-juggling activity to help students understand the importance of being organized. First, do the group juggle. When you finish the juggling activity, ask students to list the things they have to "juggle" every day. Students will list dozens of things. Then ask, "How are you able to keep up with so many things going on?" Show students how they can help themselves be better organized if they list the things they have to juggle in their student planners. They may begin to see the student planner as a way to organize school and nonschool activities like chores, part-time jobs, and church activities, as well.

Later in the school year, if a student is not keeping up with his or her assignments, reference the "juggle." Say, "You are not juggling things very well right now. Do you remember the group juggle?" Review the skills you have introduced during advisory to teach and practice organizational skills.

Setting Team Goals

Team goals act as a road map for the team. Each goal statement represents what the team wants to accomplish in a specific area. When the team members know where they want to end up, they can begin to decide on the best way to get there. With a map, you not only see where you are and where you are going, you also see what you have to go through to get there. So the team members begin their *map* as they brainstorm strategies they might employ to achieve the goal. Once the strategies are selected, the team will list the tasks to be done to achieve the goals they have selected.

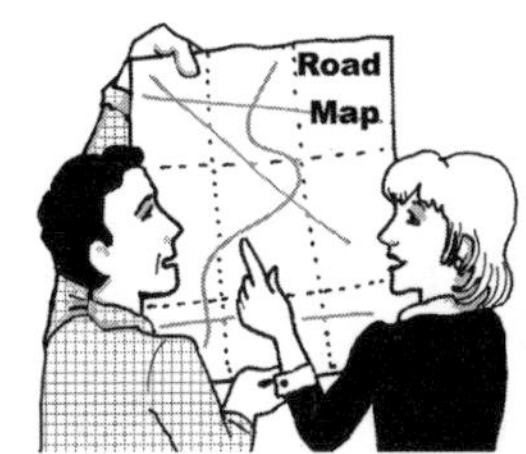

You don't run a marathon by running 26.2 miles the first week of training. If you have a personal trainer, he or she will help you plan your strategies that will include accomplishable tasks to get you ready to run the distance of a marathon. The first task is setting the goal in the first place. You have to decide that you actually want to run the marathon!

I like using the brainstorming tool below to get the team focused on each goal and the tasks that lead to achieving that goal. The idea is to target not only what tasks have to be done, but also who is responsible for the various tasks and what the timeline for each of the tasks will be.

Affective and Cognitive Goals

When a team sets goals, everyone on the team should know what they are trying to accomplish. Team goals should be measurable and should be set within the parameters of the team's ability to accomplish them. Team goals should also relate to the school's mission statement. Finally, team goals should be both *affective* as well as *cognitive*. A team should have several cognitive goals and at least one affective goal.

Affective goals relate to developing student skills such as: organizational abilities, attempting and completing assignments, participation in class, getting to classes on time, getting to school, being prepared for classes, and learning to be a peer mentor or homework partner. Actions such as helping develop the team identity and working on a service learning project would also be considered affective skills. Developing affective skills is often part of an advisory program. *(If you review Chapter 12, you will see that developing affective student skills is the primary purpose of advisory programs.)*

Affective goals also relate to developing teaching skills and parental involvement. Affective teacher skills would include working on things like: motivational skills, being a positive and productive team member, parent and student conferencing skills, providing feedback to students, making more effective parent contacts, increasing parental attendance at parent-team conferences, developing positive reinforcement systems, developing service learning projects, working toward project-based instruction, and developing alternative assessment options.

For students, cognitive goals relate to their academic performance. The team would want to look at previous test scores and base some goals on increasing the students' performance in one or more areas of the state assessments. The team might want to increase the overall team grade point average.

For teachers, cognitive goals relate to their content knowledge, how they deliver instruction, and how they assess students. The cognitive goals might include developing curriculum maps in order to create cross-curriculum learning connections, developing lessons to differentiate instruction, documenting the learning styles of the students, developing student study groups, and developing after school or lunchtime tutorial opportunities for students.

Teams should publish their goals for students, parents, the rest of the school, and the community to make them aware of the goals. I like teams to publish their team goals in their team newsletter early in the school year. That way the team can keep everyone informed about its progress via the team newsletter for the rest of the school year. The team needs to get the students, parents, the rest of the school, and the community invested in its goals. You will also see that I encourage teams to make these support groups an active part of team strategies. It is also important that the team include all of these people in its celebrations as it reaches the different goal milestones throughout the school year.

Guidelines for Team Goal Strategies

The team should develop strategies for achieving the goals that it develops. Like the goals, the strategies should be within the parameters of the team's control. It would not be practical to have a strategy of doubling the team's budget to accomplish a team goal, as the team is not in control of the school's budget. However, the team might have a strategy of fundraising as part of accomplishing a goal.

The team should be as specific as possible about the action to be taken. If fundraising is the strategy, the team would be specific about what the fundraisers would be, and how much money it hoped to raise with each event. The team outlines the tasks involved with each strategy and discusses the team members' personal responsibilities.

The strategies should be incremental so that the team can measure whether progress is being made. If the strategy involves creating displays of student work in the school and the community, the team should actually state how many displays there will be, how often student work will be displayed, the duration of the display, how the team will decide which work is to be displayed, how much work will be displayed, and a timeline for completion. That way the team can actually measure progress to the target goal at each point on the timeline.

Targeting Team Goals

This target organizer is a great tool for visualizing the team goals. The team fills out each ring. Team members add as many rings as are needed to list all of the tasks they believe are required for the goal achievement. The team decides on the timeline for each task. This timeline is often incremental, so I put the word timeline on both sides of the target. During this initial brainstorming, the team does not worry about the order of the tasks. As they think of additional tasks, they add them to the target and determine appropriate end times. The timeline provides the team with checkpoints along a goal achievement continuum.

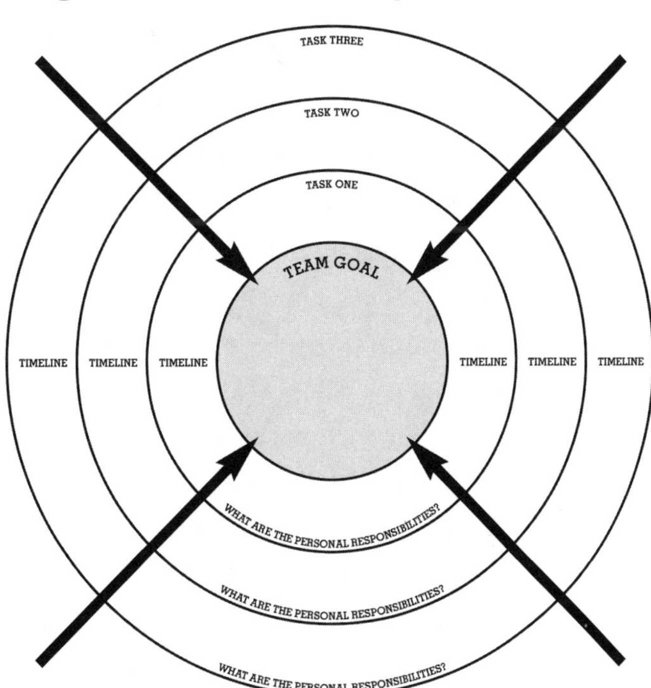

The team will also decide on and assign the personal responsibilities for each of the tasks. With each task, the person or persons responsible for that task need to be listed. As the team completes the goal achievement target, it should summarize the personal responsibilities. That way, it is clear who is supposed to do what and by when. If the personal responsibilities are not equally distributed, this will also become clear. This would be the time for the team to discuss how the personal responsibilities might be more equally distributed.

I have seen teams add several rings and even use multiple targets as they brainstormed the strategies and the tasks that would be utilized to accomplish their goals. The team then takes the information off the targets and places the tasks in chronological order. This becomes the road map the team will use throughout the school year.

I have included a few sample team goals in the charts below. Remember that the goals should be measurable.

Sample Team Cognitive Goals

- Each team member will develop at least two interdisciplinary learning connections per semester, one of which will be with an exploratory teacher.
- The team will increase reading levels of all students by at least 1.5 years.
- The team will develop at least one long-range interdisciplinary project.
- The team will develop and implement a service learning project.
- The team will increase student performance on all portions of the state assessment test by at least 10 percent.
- The team will conduct at least two pre-IEPs for each student on the team that has an IEP.
- The team will develop a curriculum-based, business-team partnership.

Sample Team Affective Goals

- The team will develop and implement one curriculum-based field trip each semester.
- The team will decrease the number of written student discipline referrals by at least 15 percent.
- The team will increase parent participation at the parent conferences by at least 20 percent.
- The team will implement an academic support system for the students.
- The team will decrease student tardiness to class by at least 15 percent.
- The team will increase student participation in the community service project by at least 10 percent.

For the sample strategies in the lists below, I have written "the team will . . ." and "the team members will . . ." on the tasks that will be involved in a variety of goals. After a team lists all of the tasks in general, team members should then go back and decide exactly who is going to be responsible for each of the tasks and when the task will be completed. Listed below each sample team goal are several sample strategies to help the team reach the goal.

Sample Team Strategies

 The team will emhasize reading across the curriculum.

- The team will use the book *How to Teach Reading When You Are Not a Reading Teacher* as a study book for the professional development portion of the team meeting time during the first marking period.
- The team will begin to implement the strategies from the book during the second marking period.
- The team will preschedule team meeting time for providing feedback and assessing the reading across the curriculum.

☆ The team will develop a tutorial program.

- Team members will rotate providing tutorial services before school, at lunch, and after school.
- The team will contact the high school for potential volunteers for providing tutorial services.
- The team will contact the parents and business community about the possibility of getting volunteers for providing tutorial services.

☆ The team will develop a curriculum-based business partnership.

- The team will contact businesses in the community to find a business to participate in the COMPASS program.
- The team will provide and explain its curriculum maps (COWs) to the business.
- Team members will develop a learning connection with the business to enhance one or more lessons and student skill development.

☆ The team will develop homework support systems.

- The team will develop a homework hotline.
- The team will develop a team website which will have homework posted each week.
- The team will use advisory time to work with students on organizational skills and to train the students how to use student planners.

☆ The team will begin Thumbs Up meetings.

- The team will conduct Thumbs Up meetings every two weeks.
- The team will add the meetings to the calendars for the team's administrators and counselors.
- The team will create the rosters from their advisory groups.
- The team will develop certificates for the students.

☆ The team will have monthly displays of student work.

- The team will create display areas for student work in the front hallway and the cafeteria.
- Each team member will call businesses until a business agrees to having student work put on display.
- Teachers will rotate the job of selecting student work for display.

☆ The team will develop a curriculum map.

- Team members will put their curriculums on the map.
- The team will dedicate three periods of team meeting time every week to integrated curriculum development.
- Team members will find learning connections and then discuss and develop them.

☆ The team will use advisory to develop the team identity.

- The team will select a theme for the school year.
- The students will decide on team identity issues during their advisory time two days a week during the first three weeks of school.
- The students will select the team name, develop the team logo, develop the team banner, decide on the team T-shirt, and decorate the team area according to the team theme and name.

☆ The team will determine the learning styles of each of their students.

- The team will use advisory time to administer instruments to determine the learning preferences of the students.
- The team will use the student learning style inventories to design more customized support for students.
- The team will use advisory time to teach students how to maximize their learning strengths in different classroom settings.

☆ Using the flexible block schedule, the team will create an extra period on their rotation. This period will be used for state test review.

- Each team member will create a state assessment review for the week of the review (the second week of each month).
- Student performance on the review assessment will be studied to identify areas needing reteaching.

Take the Planning Process to Another Level

Once the team has identified strategies it will use to reach its goals, team members will place the tasks in chronological order. Below is a sample team goal with some of the strategies the team will use to accomplish the goal. This sample shows the strategies a team developed for raising the team GPA and the tasks that must be completed to implement the strategies. This sample list also provides a space (the lines to the left of each task) for designating the person responsible for seeing progress is made. I used general timelines in the sample, such as, "in the first marking period," or "in the first semester," but your team will be more specific with the timeline.

TEAM FROG

Team Goal
The Frog Team will increase the team GPA to a 3.0 on a four-point scale.

Frog Team Strategies to Raise the Team GPA to a 3.0

1. By midsemester the team will develop homework support systems.

   ____________ The team will develop a homework hotline.

   ____________ The team will develop a team website which will have the homework posted each week.

   ____________ The team will use advisory time to work with students on organizational skills and to train the students how to use student planners.

   ____________ The team will create a homework buddy system.

   ____________ Students will be assigned homework buddies and trained in advisory during the first marking period

   ____________ Advisory groups will come together for the last ten minutes each day for homework buddies to work together.

   ____________ Homework buddies will contact each other about assignments in the event of absences.

   ____________ The team will flex the schedule to create ten minutes at the end of the day for homework buddies to meet, and then make sure students have the appropriate materials.

2. The team will assign homework every night.

____________ Team members will coordinate homework assignments during the Monday team meeting.

____________ Homework assignments will be posted in every room for every class.

____________ Combined assignments will be in the 45- to 60-minute range.

____________ Every teacher in every class will review the homework every period as a closing activity.

3. The team will adopt an evenly weighted grading policy.

____________ The team will adopt a 50-point grading system in which 0–10 = F; 11–20 = D; 21–30 = C; 31–40 = B; and 41–50 = A.

____________ The team will explain the system to students and parents during the first week of school.

A failing grade is not overemphasized as in traditional grading systems. For example, should a student receive the lowest F, which is a 0, and then a perfect score, which is the highest A (a 50), then the average would be a 25. The 25 would be a midrange C, which is what the lowest grade and highest grade should average. In the traditional grading systems, a score of 100 will average with a 0 to be a 50, which means the student still fails, even though he or she has made an A and an F, which should average to a C.

4. The team will be more flexible with learning timelines.

____________ The team will give students the opportunity to rework any assignments to correct deficiencies. Once the student demonstrates the ability to do the skills, the student will receive the appropriate grade.

____________ The teachers will provide students correctives for work done incorrectly to demonstrate how to correct the work.

____________ The late policy will be: all work must be turned in, even if late, and it will be evaluated according to its quality.

5. The team will develop a tutorial program.

    ____________ The team members will provide tutorial services before school, at lunch, and after school (rotating schedule).

    ____________ The team will contact the high school for potential volunteers for providing tutorial services.

    ____________ The team will contact the parents and business community about the possibility of getting volunteers for providing tutorial services.

6. The team will inform the parents of the team's goal to raise the team GPA to a 3.0, and enlist their support.

    ____________ The team will have an open house at the beginning of the school year to inform parents of the team expectations.

    ____________ The team will send out a monthly newsletter.

    ____________ The team will enlist the help of the parents.

    ____________ The team will share strategies for parents to help their student be successful.

    ____________ The team will enlist the support of the parents as volunteers for activities like monitoring tutoring sessions, monitoring reading groups, and chaperoning curriculum-based field experiences.

7. The team will use the Thumbs Up program to motivate students.

    ____________ The team will have Thumbs Up meetings every two weeks.

    ____________ The team will put the meetings on the calendars for the administrators and counselor for their team.

    ____________ The team will create the rosters from their advisory groups.

    ____________ The team will develop certificates for the students.

    ____________ The team will use the goal-setting sessions to help students set goals for incremental improvement in their classes.

8. The team will use the COWs to find appropriate assignments for giving students multiple grades and extra credit on at least one assignment every two weeks.

   ____________ Each teacher will develop at least two opportunities each marking period for giving students an additional grade and extra credit for work done in some other teacher's class.

   ____________ At least one of the opportunities for giving students an additional grade and extra credit each semester will be for work done in one or more of the exploratory classes.

9. The team will develop a curriculum-based business partnership.

   ____________ The team will contact businesses in the community to procure a business to participate in the COMPASS program.

   ____________ The team will provide and explain the curriculum maps (COWs) to the business.

   ____________ The team members will develop a learning connection with the business to enhance one or more lessons and student skill development.

   ____________ The business partners will work with the students to emphasize quality and timely work.

   ____________ The business partners will provide some tutorial assistance.

10. The team will have a motivational opening team meeting with all the students to demonstrate the teachers' expectations and the students' responsibilities.

11. The team will have monthly displays of student work.

    ____________ The team will create display areas for student work in the front hallway and the cafeteria.

    ____________ Each team member will call businesses until a business agrees to arrange having student work put on display.

    ____________ Teachers will rotate getting student work for display from their classes.

12. The team will create a weekly team calendar with all assignments during the Monday team meeting.

    ____________ The team calendar and daily assignments will be posted on the team's website.

    ____________ The team will have the team calendar posted in the team hallway and copies will be in each teacher's classroom.

13. The team will teach the importance and use of student planners.

    ____________ Do the group-juggle during the orientation in the first week of school in advisory groups.

    ____________ The student's advisor will work with the students daily to ensure the appropriate use of the student planners.

14. The team will implement a system for positive reinforcements to recognize students' efforts and achievements.

    ____________ The Thumbs Up system will be used.

    ____________ The team will use a variety of point and ticket systems for students to earn various rewards, including a team field day.

15. The team will have at least one curriculum-based field experience each semester.

Team Goal Assessment

The team should plan to assess their progress toward their goals at least once a month. Team goal assessment should be a prescheduled team-meeting topic. For example, the team could assess its progress toward the goals the first Monday of each month. At this time the team can measure the progress toward goal achievement and make adjustments as needed. On occasion, the team may see that the goal could be accomplished sooner that had been predicted. Of course, there are also times that this is not the case, and the team may need to adjust the timeline or the strategies that they are implementing. Either way, the team can revisit the initial timelines and all new strategies, and adjust previous ones. Teachers are accustomed to monitoring and adjusting situations that present themselves in educational settings. Assessing goal achievement on a regular basis allows the team opportunities for monitoring, adjusting, and refocusing as needed.

TAG . . . You're It!

Establishing Goals

Exercise One

Work with your team to develop one cognitive goal. Use the guidelines in the chapter to make sure the goal is measurable and that it will impact student performance. Brainstorm the strategies that your team is going to employ to reach the established goal. Your team might want to use the goal achievement target, or you might just list the strategies. Each strategy will involve one or more tasks, and the team should list the personal responsibilities for each of the tasks listed. Remember to determine the timeline for each of the strategies and the corresponding tasks. Finally, your team should decide how often they are going to assess the goal they are tracking progress toward.

Exercise Two

Work with your team to develop one affective goal. Follow the guidelines in the chapter as you did when you wrote your cognitive goal.

Exercise Three

Your team should establish at least two cognitive goals and one affective goal. This is your chance to complete your team's personal roadmap to success.

Teaming to Increase Student Test Scores

Score Big and Win at High-stakes Testing!

Teams can make a huge difference in student performance on state assessments. Working in departments, schools can impact test scores by improving curriculum alignment, adjusting timelines, developing common assessments, and embedding assessment items modeled after state assessments. However, departmental strategies can only go so far. When the school community as a whole becomes involved and departments share strategies, test scores can reach the highest levels possible. Interdepartmental sharing (teaming) means developing an interdisciplinary approach to curriculum development to complement and supplement the departmental work.

The optimum way to maximize interdisciplinary teaching and assessment is through teams. Teams generally set a variety of goals, but in today's educational climate almost every team has at least one goal relating to optimizing the test scores. Every strategy utilized by high-performing teams will, directly or indirectly, have some impact on students' performance on state assessments. For example, reducing discipline problems allows for more instructional time. Some strategies that directly impact state assessment scores are team tests, shared assessments, portfolios, parent packets, remediation and enrichment options, advisory activities, and Targeted Extended Support for Teachers and Students (T.E.S.T.S.). *(Every strategy shared in this book will ultimately impact student test scores, but this chapter focuses on team strategies that improve test scores.)*

Getting Ready for the Big Game Means Practice, Practice, Practice

Team tests are a great way for students to practice and become familiar with the test format for state tests. While this should never be the primary focus of assessment, we do need to create opportunities for students to get familiar with the state assessment format. Using released items from the state tests, and teacher-made test items created in the same format as the state test items, departments can create assessments for each unit of instruction. These assessments can be used before units of instruction as pretests, during units as a part of instruction, and as summative evaluations.

Anytime one of the teachers on the team is ready to give a pre- or posttest, the rest of the team can help. The team can administer the test together. For a discussion of how this format is "brain appropriate," see Chapter 10, Flexing the Schedule. An example of how to modify the team's schedule to accommodate a common assessment is given in that chapter. The teacher "giving" the test makes enough copies for everyone on the team. The students are assigned to one of the teachers for taking the test. Then, the teachers on the team use the first part of their instructional block to administer the test to all of the students at the same time (in the same format as state tests).

Large group tests become a normal part of student activities, so that taking the state assessments is just another assessment day. We want students to feel as comfortable as possible when taking the state tests and nothing makes a student more comfortable than familiarity and confidence. The practice of teams regularly administering common assessments guarantees that students will be familiar with the testing format, and less anxious about the state tests when they happen.

When visiting schools, I like to ask about how they administer their state tests. For example, I want to know how they group the students and what time of day they administer the tests. Of course, you know the common answers to those questions. The students generally take the state assessments first thing in the mornings over a period of several days. The students are usually in the same room, most often their homeroom, in the mornings for the days of the tests, regardless of what the topics of the test are on any given days. The students are in unfamiliar groupings for most of the test areas. For example, students may have the English teacher for homeroom, which means they will be taking the math portion of the state test with their homeroom group rather than their math class.

How many other tests are administered in that format during the school year? Occasionally, schools will administer a practice test to help get students ready for the state testing format, but more often than not, this is a completely new experience. Schools regularly wait until time for the high-stakes tests to coach parents and students about test-taking strategies such as getting the students to bed early on the test days.

Great teams use their newsletters and parent meetings to inform their parents about their team assessment days throughout the year. The teachers encourage their parents to do things like make sure their students get a good night's sleep, bring the appropriate materials, and have a good breakfast prior to the assessment. If common team assessment times are part of a team's plan for test preparation, taking the state tests will not be a new and different experience, but one students have experienced many times.

One concern with administering team common assessments is that if the teacher giving the assessment is the expert, the other teachers may not know how to help students should they have questions about items on the assessment. The other teachers don't know if the teacher responsible for the assessment gives the students any assistance. Here is one way to deal with that concern.

When team members plan a team common assessment, they also contact the administrative team. The administrative team provides coverage for the teacher who wrote the assessment. That teacher rotates between the rooms while the assessment is being given. Students can ask questions when the teacher rotates through their room.

I encourage teams and schools to do the same thing when administering the state assessments. That is, they should work out coverage for the teachers that teach whatever area is being administered at any one time. These teachers can rotate through as students take the portion of the state test that deals with their subject. While teachers are absolutely not allowed to provide any assistance to the students during the state assessment, just seeing the social studies teacher helps visual learners; hearing the social studies teacher's voice helps auditory learners; and having the social studies teacher walk through the room helps the kinesthetic learners. In this way, the social studies teacher helps students without providing any direct assistance.

Shared Assessments

Working together to give common team assessments has another advantage when the team is developing an interdisciplinary approach to delivering instruction. In the discussion of the COW as a tool for finding learning connections between content areas, I mention how to attach sample state test items to the COWs to determine when they would be used. By helping administer each other's tests, teachers can better determine when those test items might be cross-referenced and best used in multiple areas.

A team's eventual goal might be to make sure that exploratory classes have imbedded assessment items from other curriculum areas. In this way the students will have the opportunity to apply their skills in various settings, and answer the exact same questions as they reappear on multiple tests in multiple areas. This repetition enhances the students' retention of the skills, and their ability to apply those skills in variety of circumstances.

As teachers become more familiar with the COWs and sharing assessment items through learning connections, the students will begin to see the same assessment items showing up on multiple assessments with much more regularity. This interdisciplinary approach is a natural way to expose the students to the various skills and assessment items multiple times in multiple areas within the building.

Remember, it is crucial to involve the exploratory and elective teachers when developing learning connections and sharing test items. Occasionally, some exploratory teachers are assigned to teams on a rotating basis. In that situation, the exploratory teacher can also assist in the administering of the team common assessments. *(Don't forget, instead of doing a "skill of the day" which may or may not be in the context of the rest of the day, teachers can reinforce each other's skills and test items when they "fit naturally" into their area.)*

Creating Portfolios

High-performing teams have their students create portfolios to document progress with ongoing interdisciplinary projects and mastery of the skills associated with the state standards. Portfolio management is usually done during advisory time. The advisor works with each student to select copies of assessments and other documentation showing mastery of the state standards. As the students work with their portfolios to decide what piece of work will demonstrate a specific skill, the students also become more familiar with the skills. Seeing their work accumulate also builds confidence for the students. Every time students open their portfolios to review them or add new work, they are reminded of the previous skills achieved. The yearlong "bid writing" project described in Chapter 3, Interdisciplinary Curriculum Development, demonstrates the use of portfolios as a tool to manage the materials as an interdisciplinary project develops.

The portfolio can be as simple as a file folder with the student's name on it that is kept in an advisor's room. List the state standards on the outside of the folder, and have the student check off each standard when something is added that demonstrates mastery of that particular skill or set of skills. Advisors should review the portfolios regularly with their students, and help the students stay current. Advisors who have shared assessment items and worked on the COWs have an advantage because they are more familiar with the kind of work the students are doing in the other classes.

If your school runs student-led conferences, teachers are already familiar with helping the students accumulate examples of work to share with their parents during the conferences. In addition to sending home report cards, many teams send home information about students' progress on their portfolios. It can be easy to keep parents up-to-date about where their students are in regard to being prepared for the upcoming state tests.

If each department puts together sets of examples to demonstrate each of the state standards, the advisor can send home practice packets for the parents and students as needed. Some schools have enrichment or seminar periods to provide additional support for students. Portfolios help teachers in those periods determine what the students need to work on, so the enrichment or seminar periods do not become additional study halls. *(We all know what happens or, more to the point, what does not happen in study hall periods.)*

Targeted Support in Enrichment Periods

In the discussion of flexible scheduling (Chapter 10), you learned how teams can create an extra period by using a rotating-drop schedule. Each teacher can create a curriculum-based activity that would not otherwise fit into the regular schedule. Another use for adding the extra period could be for enrichment or extension activities. Every student can participate in an extended learning opportunity.

Portfolios are a good way to target appropriate placement of students in enrichment groups. Team members can identify which enrichment activities will benefit each of the students. The team will determine which teachers can provide enrichment in each area. When teams create a period of time for enrichment, they can target appropriate instruction to specific skills for specific groups.

Any teacher that has been able to put assessment items for a skill on one or more of their tests can also provide enrichment for students for those particular standards. That means that if students need enrichment for a particular math standard, they may be assigned to a shop teacher, an art teacher, or a science teacher. As the enrichment process progresses, the portfolio becomes the place for students and teachers to put any work that demonstrates the students' mastery, or at least the students' attempts at mastering skills. So, the mastery of a math concept might be shown by work the student has done with the art teacher.

The advisor can make assignments to the enrichment time based on progress demonstrated with each student's portfolio. Also, other teachers might assign students to certain enrichment classes based on what is happening in their classes.

Parent Support

One of the things I encourage departments to do is develop a few extra activities, practice-test items, or other work for each of the state standards. These packets can be shared with parents of students who need extra assistance. As teams review students' progress, they may enlist the help of the parents. With the prepared packets, teachers are able to target the assistance the parents are going to give their students. Teachers can emphasize the critical role parents play as a part of the relay team that is sharing in the responsibility for their students' success. Set up a parent conference to enlist the help of the parents. *(Getting to the finish line requires a team effort, and if we want to be able to pass a baton on to the parents, we need to have something to pass along to them.)*

Advisory Strategies

There are many activities that can be done during advisory time to enhance students' performance on the state assessments. Besides helping students develop portfolios, advisors can work on affective skills required for maximizing cognitive achievement. In addition to teaching organizational and listening skills, advisors can work specifically on the test-taking skills. Many resource books and materials are available to assist teachers with these skills. *Learning to Learn* is a great activity-based study skills book for teachers. *Fire Up for Learning!* is full of challenging and motivating activities for students that teach such skills as following directions, how to focus, and active listening.

Putting It All Together for T.E.S.T.S.

Since everything in education needs an acronym, I thought what better acronym than T.E.S.T.S., as everything teachers and schools do seems to revolve around those state assessments! T.E.S.T.S. stands for Targeted Extended Support for Teachers and Students.

Any teacher can get extended support for their efforts with COWs. Teachers can identify learning connections which target specific skills they teach as they are being used in other classes. Teachers then get targeted support in the form of additional examples from the other classes to demonstrate skills they are teaching. As they develop learning connections, multiple teachers target and reinforce the same skills. Assessment items are repeated on different tests for additional reinforcement, which increases students' retention of the skills. So, the COWs are great tools for helping teachers provide targeted support for each other.

The COWs are also very good tools to promote business and community partnerships. COMPASS stands for Community Partnerships Assuring Student Success, and the purpose of the program is to find community resources that might be available to help teachers with specific lessons. In Chapter 4, COMPASS, I discuss how businesses can also use the COWs to help teachers. All business assistance is targeted to specific topics and skills.

By cross-referencing skills and assessment items on the COWs, teachers are able to target additional support for students as needed. The science teacher may have students getting extended support from a variety of other teachers, depending on the skills they are working on at any given time. If the school has an advisory program, the students get additional extended support for developing the affective skills necessary for cognitive success. Using the portfolios, the advisor can target specific areas of concern for a student, along with the appropriate support systems to help that student put together a game plan for success.

Therefore, T.E.S.T.S. is the combination of all of the systems and strategies shared in *Get Fit*. Not only do teachers and students receive extended support—that support is targeted to specific needs. In many schools there are also programs such as SAP (Student Assistance Program) or SAT (Student Assistance Team). The purpose of these programs is to coordinate efforts for students in need of support. The idea of T.E.S.T.S. is to create systems of support for both teachers and students that overlap and intertwine into a web of support that leaves no teacher or student behind. This is the coordination of the opportunities for collaboration to maximize the efforts of everyone in the school and community to meet the needs of all teachers and students.

Hopefully, this book proves that you do not have to teach like the test—or to the test—to teach for the test. I believe that every administrator, teacher, and parent should follow this guideline:

I will not lower
my standards
to raise yours.
!

TAG . . . You're It!

Increasing Test Scores

Exercise One

Identify the various support systems that are available in your school. Then discuss how you are currently using the available support systems, and how you might better coordinate your efforts. Remember that your team should identify the support systems available for teachers as well as for students. Ask, "Do the support systems in place provide support for every teacher and for every student?"

Exercise Two

After your team has identified and discussed the current support systems in place, then discuss adding new support systems. Each support system should complement and supplement the others. Create your own T.E.S.T.S. to ensure that every teacher and student receives support that targets their needs.

Appendix

Name: ______________________ Week of: ______________________

Date	Student	Parent/Guardian	Phone Conversation

PLANNING CHART

WHO? WHEN? WHAT?

Connecting Areas, Weeks, Timeline, and Topics

STUDENT WORK

Focus Activities, Reference Points, Shared Assignments, Assessments

STANDARDS ADDRESSED

What questions will be answered?

DIFFERENTIATION IN EVIDENCE

Shared Strategies, Multiple Intelligences, Learning Styles, and Modalities

Integrated Curriculum and Learning Connections

PLANNING CHART

WHO? WHEN? WHAT?

Connecting Areas, Weeks, Timeline, and Topics

STUDENT WORK

Focus Activities, Reference Points, Shared Assignments, Assessments

STANDARDS ADDRESSED

What questions will be answered?

DIFFERENTIATION IN EVIDENCE

Shared Strategies, Multiple Intelligences, Learning Styles, and Modalities

Positive Reinforcements and Rewards Record

Student Behavior

Reinforcements, Accommodations, and Rewards Available

Date	Rewards Offered	Result

COMMUNITY SERVICE LEARNING LOG

DATE	HOURS	LOCATION OF SERVICE	TYPE OF SERVICE	SERVICE SUPERVISOR

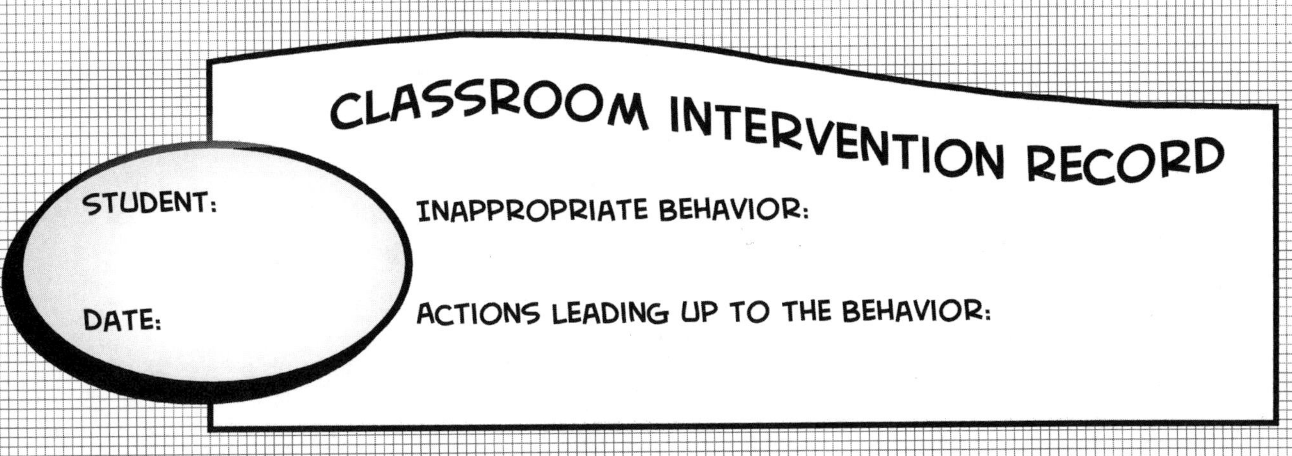

DATE	INTERVENTION ATTEMPTED	RESULT

ADDITIONAL INTERVENTIONS AVAILABLE

TEAM INTERVENTION RECORD

STUDENT:

DATE:

INAPPROPRIATE BEHAVIOR:

ACTIONS LEADING UP TO THE BEHAVIOR:

DATE	INTERVENTION ATTEMPTED	RESULT

ADDITIONAL INTERVENTIONS AVAILABLE

References and Selected Readings

Suggested Readings for Advisory Programs

Books from Incentive Publications:

Advisory Plus
Character Education Years One and Two
Character Education Book of Plays
Middle School Matters
Fire Up for Learning!
Learning to Learn
It Takes Character
Risk It!

From the NMSA

Clair Cole *Nurturing a Teacher Advisory Program* (1992)
James, Michael, and Nancy Spradling *Advisory to Advocacy: Meeting Every Student's Needs* (2001)

Additional References and Suggested Readings

Daniel H. Pink *A Whole New Mind* (2006) The Berkley Publishing Group 1-57322-308-5

Robert Kriegel *If it ain't broke . . . Break It!* (1991) Warner Books, Inc.

Robert Kriegel *Sacred Cows Make the Best Burgers* (1996) Warner Books Inc.

Peter Kline & Bernard Saunders *Ten Steps to a Learning Organization* (1993) Great Ocean Publishers, Inc.

Darrel Ray & Howerd Bronstein *Teaming Up* (1995) McGraw Hill, Inc.

R. Bruce Willians & Steven E. Dunn Brain Compatible Learning for the Block ((2000) Skylight Training and Publishing, Inc.

Peggy A. Hammeken *Inclusion: 450 Strategies for Success* (1995) Peytral Publications

Marcia Conti-D'Antonio, Robert Bertrando, Joanne Eisenberger *Supporting Students With Learning Needs In The Block* (1998) Eye On Education

Barbara A. Lewis *The Kid's Guide to Social Action* (1991) Free Spirit Publishing, Inc.

Jacobe, H.H. *Mapping the Big Picture: Integrating Curriculum and Assessment K-12* (1997) Alexandria, VA. Association for Supervision and Curriculum Development

Udelofen, S. *Keys to Curriculum Mapping: Strategies and Tools to Make It Work.* Thousand Oaks, CA: Corwin Press

From Incentive Publications:

The Definitive Middle School
WOW, What A Team!
Including the Special Needs Child
Success With IEPs
How to Write a Successful IEP

From the NMSA:

Turning Points 2000: Education Adolescents in the 21st Century
Vincent Anfara and Sandra Stacki *Middle School Curriculum, Instruction, and Assessment* (2002)
Edited by Ann Lockledge and Judith Hayn *Using Portfolios Across the Curriculum* (200)
Miki Caskey *Making a Difference: Action Research in Middle Level Education* (2005)
Research and Resource in Support of This We Believe (2003)